Assessing Minority Students with Learning and Behavior Problems

D0828045

Catherine Collier

Hamilton Publications
Lindale, Texas

LC 3719
C64x

ISBN: 0-940059-05-3

Library of Congress Catalog Card Number: 88-81254

Contents

Preface

Assessment is the systematic process of gathering information to make decisions about the education of students. It is often employed to identify students with learning and behavior problems and their particular special learning needs. Appropriate, accurate assessment and identification of special needs students from culturally and linguistically different backgrounds have been a complex problem for educators not only because of the students' diverse backgrounds but because assessment itself is difficult and far from an exact science. In regard to assessing minority students, professionals have believed for many years that the usual assessment procedures and instruments are inappropriate. However, knowledge of students' behavioral, cognitive, and academic strengths and weaknesses is necessary for developing appropriate instruction. It is important for teachers to know if a minority student's learning and behavior problems are a temporary function of his or her level of acculturation and language acquisition or an indication of a more serious handicapping condition.

This book focuses upon practical and appropriate assessment procedures while providing a foundation in the sociocultural elements which must be considered in implementing these procedures with minority students. Section I provides a discussion of minority students in today's schools, including legal concerns, as well as detailed descriptions of the five major sociocultural factors to consider in assessing minority students. Section II provides an in-depth discussion of the use of different assessment techniques for gathering information about sociocultural factors. We will address a number of informal as well as formal assessment techniques with primary attention paid to the informal procedures. Section III provides a description of the assessment process, emphasizing the referral, staffing, and placement stages of assessment, and highlights specific considerations to be addressed when assessing culturally and linguistically different learners.

The primary emphasis is on the identification and assessment of sociocultural factors which permeate various learning or behavior problems of minority students. Although several major aspects associated with the assessment process are explored, the emphasis is upon assessment for instruction at the classroom level. The discussions in this book emphasize practical recommendations and suggestions; however, an overview of the theoretical and research foundation for these recommendations and suggestions is also provided. This book is written for practicing teachers, diagnosticians, school psychologists, and other education professionals who are involved in assessing the special needs of minority students from diverse cultural and linguistic backgrounds who exhibit learning and behavior problems. Preservice teachers and diagnosticians in training should also find this book useful as they prepare for their careers. Throughout this book, the terms "minority," "culturally diverse," and "linguistically different" are used interchangeably. The focus is upon the student from a bilingual, limited English speaking, culturally and/or linguistically diverse or different sociocultural background. The author wishes to express appreciation to those professionals who reviewed this manuscript during various stages of development. Their insightful comments and suggestions were most helpful in the preparation of this book.

C. C.

SECTION I
INTRODUCTION TO ASSESSING MINORITY STUDENTS

Improved assessment capabilities and identification of students' instructional needs are critical for minority populations. Discussion in this section provides a brief overview of culturally and linguistically different populations, of the controversy concerning minority assessment, and of the legal regulations which currently pertain to minority assessment and placement in special education. This section concludes with a description of the five major sociocultural factors which must be considered when assessing minority students: cultural and linguistic background, experiential background, the stage and pattern of acculturation, patterns of sociolinguistic development and language transfer, and culturally different cognitive and learning styles.

Minority Students in Today's Schools

The population of minority students in this country is increasing steadily and will continue to be a concern to educators for many years. Among these students are those who have special learning and behavior problems, some of which may be due to the presence of handicapping conditions. There are approximately 500,000 handicapped students aged 5 to 12 years from non-English language backgrounds (Baca & Cervantes, in press).

Often, special education students with language or cultural differences do not have their language needs met, either through English as a Second Language (ESL) instruction or other alternative approaches. The Education of All Handicapped Children's Act (P.L. 94-142) requires that an Individual Education Plan (IEP) be developed for each student in the language best understood by the student and parents. However, if the school district cannot meet the language and cultural needs of the exceptional student due to lack of resources or staff trained in bilingual special education, such services for the student may not be considered.

It is of paramount importance that these students

2

be identified early and their unique learning needs be addressed as effectively and comprehensively as possible. Some learning and behavior problems may be due to the students' different sociolinguistic and cultural backgrounds, their adjustment to a new sociocultural milieu, the presence of a handicapping condition, or the combined effects of these situations.

The learning and behavior problems exhibited by minority students are often similar to the problems which elicit referrals for all students (e.g., lack of or seriously deficient academic achievement, social and classroom behavior which is disruptive to instruction, or other problems difficult for the teacher to handle in the general classroom setting). One major difference between the minority and the mainstream students who exhibit these behaviors lies in the interaction (or lack thereof) among cultural and sociolinguistic factors and a suspected handicap (e.g., learning disability, mental retardation, emotional disturbance). The level of interaction also affects decisions concerning the most effective intervention for resolution of the problem.

An observer of Mary and Maria, for example, may see very similar manifestations of learning and behavior problems in both students. They both may be performing at two to three levels below their peers in reading and writing, they both may seem distracted and inattentive to classroom activities, and both may act out disruptive behaviors whenever the teacher changes the instructional environment. These are all real learning and behavior problems which must be addressed by the classroom teacher and may require the assistance of other education specialists. However, while special education placement may be of benefit to Mary, a more appropriate instructional intervention for Maria may include intensive first and second language development, cross-cultural communication strategies, assistance in dealing with stress due to acculturation, and curriculum adaptation to meet her cultural and sociolinguistic differences.

Changes in the traditional assessment process are necessary to determine the most appropriate instructional response to Maria's learning and behavior problems. Learning and behavior problems that seem to be indicative of a handicapping condition may actually be the manifestation of cultural and sociolinguistic differences, or may indicate problems related to both cultural and linguistic factors and a handicapping condition. When assessing learning and behavior problems in minority student populations, we must consider these possibilities and the legal requirements in minority student assessment.

Controversial Issues in Minority Assessment

There is much controversy about assessment in general and about assessment of minority students in particular. Professionals in the field of bilingual/ESL education have concluded that many of the assessment procedures used with minority students are ethically questionable and politically motivated (Baca & Cervantes, in press; Cummins, 1984). Assessment procedures for placement and programming of any student are not considered very cost-effective. In addition, assessment results may be irrelevant to programming and may merely confirm the initial impressions of the classroom teacher (Ysseldyke & Algozzine, 1982). Often, placement and programming outcomes of special education assessments are determined by the teacher's initial referral rather than by the results of formal assessment (Collier, 1985; Ysseldyke & Algozzine, 1981).

As characterized by Ysseldyke and Algozzine (1982), the decision to provide services in special education is often the result of vague and subjective referrals based on subjective variables and inconsistent, indefensible criteria. Students are often tested automatically with inappropriate instruments. This characterization of current assessment limitations is even more egregious for minority students. The average exceptional student's assessment may last 13 to 15 hours; by the time the decision-making process is completed, the cost could be as much as $1,800 (Ysseldyke & Algozzine, 1982). The time and special personnel required to screen and assess minority students place additional stress on school district funds and resources.

This is frequently true when assessment results are not used to make either placement or programming decisions. In the studies reported by Ysseldyke, Algozzine, Richey, and Graden (1982), very little correlation was found between the decisions made and the extent to which the assessment data supported the decisions. An analysis of staffing meetings indicated that 83% of the oral comments were irrelevant to federal and state criteria for placement and were not used for programming development or eligibility even when they contained relevant information. In essence, recommended and instructionally meaningful criteria are not used to guide the assessment process. In addition, there is concern that characteristics such as physical appearance, levels of acculturation, or differences in sociolinguistic or cultural background may influence placement and programming (Hoover & Collier, 1985).

Gathering and analyzing socioculturally relevant information about minority students with learning and behavior problems facilitate placement and programming decisions. Besides gathering information about the learning and behavior problems of minority students, assessment personnel should also gather specific sociocultural information. Indeed, information about sociocultural factors and their contribution to the student's learning and behavior problems must be obtained prior to referral for formal evaluation. Appropriate placement and programming decisions should be made with knowledge of the extent to which sociocultural factors contribute to the learning and behavior problems of a minority student. This consideration in the formal assessment process helps schools meet legal

5

requirements for minority student assessment. Specific sociocultural factors to consider are discussed in a later section. At this time we will discuss key legal requirements related to the assessment of minority students.

Legal Requirements

The identification and assessment of culturally and linguistically different students who may be handicapped has been the subject of legislation for many years. This has led to several legal guidelines that must be followed when minority students are assessed. The cases of <u>Dyrcia S. et al. v. Board of Education of the City of New York et al.</u> (1979), <u>Larry P. v. Riles</u> (1979), and <u>Jose P. v. Ambach</u> (1979) are very significant because they addressed both the cultural and sociolinguistic needs and the special education needs of minority students. Pertinent recommendations resulting from this and other litigation are summarized by Baca and Cervantes (in press) and include the following:

1. Identification of students who need special education services must include the use of adequate bilingual resources.

2. Appropriate evaluation must include the establishment of school-based support teams to evaluate students in their own environment using a bilingual nondiscriminatory evaluation process.

3. Appropriate programs in the least restrictive environment must include a comprehensive continuum of services with the provision of appropriate bilingual programs at each level of the continuum for students with limited English proficiency.

4. Due process and parental student rights must include a native language version of a parents' rights booklet, which explains all of the due

6

process rights of students and parents. Also included is the hiring of neighborhood workers to facilitate parental involvement in the evaluation and development of the individualized educational program.

Many regulations based on educational and civil rights legislation have been developed to protect the rights of culturally and linguistically different and exceptional students. Regulations which are especially pertinent to the assessment of minority students include the following:

1. A language screening should be conducted at the beginning of each school year to determine if the new students are exposed to or influenced by a language other than English (Lau v. Nichols, 414 U.S. 563; 39 L. Ed. 2d 1, 945. Ct. 786; 1974).

2. If this initial language screening indicates the presence of a language other than English, an assessment of language dominance and proficiency should be conducted (Lau v. Nichols).

3. Parents must be informed of all due process rights in their native or most proficient language. An interpreter must be provided at all meetings if parents cannot communicate effectively in English (Title VI, Civil Rights Act, U.S.C. 200d 1964; P. L. 95-561 92 Stat. 2268 Elementary and Secondary Education Amendments 1978 (ESEA); The Education of All Handicapped Children's Act, P. L. 94-142, 1975).

4. Tests and other evaluation materials must be validated for their intended purpose and administered by trained personnel according to the instructions of the test designers (P. L. 94-142).

5. The assessment instruments must be linguistically and culturally appropriate and testing shall be

conducted in a nondiscriminatory manner (P. L.
94-142; Section 504 of the Rehabilitation Act,
1973).

6. Tests are to be selected and administered in a
   manner that insures that test results accurately
   reflect the aptitude or achievement level (or
   whatever the test purports to measure) of
   students with limited language skills rather than
   their limited language skills (P. L. 94-142;
   Section 504).

7. When analyzing evaluation data for placement
   decisions, information shall be drawn from a
   variety of sources, including socioeconomic and
   cultural background, and adaptive behavior (P. L.
   94-142; Section 504).

8. If it is determined that a minority student is
   handicapped and has limited English proficiency,
   an IEP which reflects the student's language and
   culture needs shall be developed (P. L. 94-142;
   Section 504 of the Rehabilitation Act, 1973;
   Title VI; Title VII, P. L. 95-561).

Besides addressing these legal guidelines,
assessment practitioners should consider
sociocultural factors that are important in the
assessment of minority students.

Sociocultural Considerations When Assessing Minority Students

Areas of special concern in the assessment of
minority students include five sociocultural
factors: cultural and linguistic background,
experiential background, the stage and pattern of
acculturation, patterns of sociolinguistic
development and language transfer, and cognitive and
learning styles. These are the foundation for the
assessment and instruction of culturally and
linguistically different students. Addressing these

8

five sociocultural factors will help the practitioner ascertain whether the learning and behavior problems exhibited by the minority student are due to either sociocultural factors, some other problem or disability, or a combination of these. This type of assessment will raise "red flags" which indicate that sociocultural factors are causing the minority student's learning and behavior problems. The absence of "red flags" indicates a high probability that sociocultural factors are not the primary cause for the problems, though they cannot be ruled out completely. The five areas of special concern in the assessment of minority students are discussed in the ensuing paragraphs.

Cultural and Linguistic Background

All human beings grow up within a cultural context. The process of acquiring one's native culture is called enculturation and may begin in the womb. Adapting to a different culture is called acculturation. "Culture consists of whatever it is one has to know or believe in order to operate in a manner acceptable to its members" (Goodenough, 1957, p. 167). Culture is how we organize our behaviors, communication, values, and emotions; it is the patterns of interaction, communication, socialization, and education held in common by a particular group of people.

The components of culture—language, behavior, and socialization—are not static but are changed continually by the influence of both internal and external circumstances. Where several cultures are in contact, where there is much movement and communication between social groups and geographic areas, some overlapping and blurring of cultural boundaries will occur. However, it is true that both enculturation and acculturation shape an individual's cultural identity.

The way individuals perceive, relate to, and interpret their environment is shaped by their cultural milieu. Culture determines how we think (cognition), how we interact (behavior), how we communicate (language) and how we transmit knowledge to the next generation (education) (Collier & Hoover, 1987). Since culture has such a comprehensive effect upon the thinking, perceptions, and interaction patterns of individuals, practitioners must become familiar with the cultural and sociolinguistic background of their students, particularly students with learning and behavior problems. Our educational system is founded on culturally based assumptions about what students should learn, how and where they should learn it, as well as why and when they will need this knowledge. Students reared in a different cultural environment will have learned a different body of knowledge and will have learned it in different ways. Education professionals must be sensitive to the cultural and sociolinguistic backgrounds of minority students and must consider how these differences may affect a student's performance during the assessment process.

Experiential Background

Differences in experience may account for much of the discrepancy between achievement and ability seen in minority students with learning and behavior problems. Many refugee and immigrant students in this country come from socioeconomic and political situations where they have not had the educational experiences of mainstream American students (Nazarro, 1981). This is also true of many Hispanic and Native American students, especially those who live in migrant families (Serrano, 1982). Many of these students are raised in settings with little or no exposure to regular and consistent public school education or to children's educational programs such as day care centers and educational television. As a result, many minority students lack experiences and preskills which are important for learning in American public schools, and which are frequently incorporated into public school assessment.

Differences in experiential background also

affect minority students' responses to various elements of the curriculum. The use of inquiry techniques, behavior contracting, active processing and other individualized instructional strategies is very dependent on prior experience. Role expectations and the ability to make quick cause-and-effect associations are necessary prerequisite skills for optimal effectiveness of many strategies. Minority students' lack of appropriate response to these commonly used instructional strategies compounds their learning and behavior problems and may be mistaken as an indication of a handicapping condition.

Some of the minority students' responses to the school environment may be due to previous school experiences and others to cultural differences. Students who have been in school systems in other countries generally know basic school procedures, such as raising their hands for attention, asking permission to do something, and recess and lunchroom behaviors. However, they may be unfamiliar with particular instructional strategies, such as independent or silent reading rather than group recitation, or discovery learning rather than rote memorization. Their inappropriate responses to silent reading, discovery learning, or other activities may be disruptive or troublesome to the teacher and can result in a referral.

Minority students with no school experience may be unfamiliar with particular instructional strategies as well as the basic operational expectations of the school and classroom. They may not know how or when to ask for assistance or permission, may not be familiar with appropriate school behavior in or out of the classroom, and may not have had any exposure to academic language. These students may need to acculturate not only to American culture but also to the culture of the school itself.

In addition to these experience-based responses to the school environment, differences in school behavior may be due to cultural differences. For example, many cultures value group process over individual achievement. More value is placed on individual contribution to the success of the group than on success of the individual. A student who appears to act apart from the group may be shunned or ridiculed in many Native American and Asian cultures (Hoover & Collier, 1985; Nazarro, 1981; Woodward, 1981). Since much of the assessment conducted to identify learning and behavior problems isolates and singles out the individual student, assessment may in fact compound the student's problems in the classroom and in the home. The fear of being seen by peers as different may affect the student's performance during individually administered assessment procedures. During group assessment, the minority student may be concerned about assisting other students and not very concerned about personal performance.

Additionally, minority students from a culture that values indirectness and distance as evidence of appropriate behavior may not respond positively to the use of touching or praise as reinforcement strategies. These students' interpretation of "time out" and other teaching and behavior management techniques may be quite different from the teacher's intent when utilizing those techniques. Inappropriate responses may lead the teacher to suspect the presence of a handicapping condition.

Differences in response to the school environment need to be analyzed to determine if they are really examples of cultural diversity. If it is established clearly that the student's inappropriate behavior in the school is not due to cultural differences or to lack of school experience, the teacher may proceed with the analysis of other possible causes, including the presence of a handicapping condition. Experiential differences affect both classroom behavior and performance on assessment devices. Practitioners who work with minority students need to be aware of and be able to identify experiential differences in order to improve the assessment and instruction of minority students.

Acculturation

Educators who work with minority students who have learning and behavior problems also need to address the effects of acculturation. The minority student's cultural identity is affected by both enculturation and acculturation. The common concept of acculturation is the "melting pot," the assimilation of one cultural group into another. However, assimilation is but one element of the complex process of acculturation.

Acculturation is the process of adaptation to a new cultural environment. When the native culture is essentially eliminated from the person's cognitive behavior as the second culture takes its place, we say assimilation has occurred. This acculturative response is actually rather rare; a person more frequently integrates new cultural patterns into the cognitive and behavioral framework of the first culture. This more common response to the acculturative process usually results in better mental health (Szapocznik & Kurtines, 1980).

Of special concern to education professionals are the psychological responses to the acculturation experience which are very similar to indicators of handicapping conditions. These include confused locus of control, heightened anxiety, poor self-image, and withdrawal (Collier, 1985; Padilla, 1980). Another effect of acculturation is acculturative stress. This stress is common, though not inevitable, during acculturation. Berry (1970) states that acculturative stress is characterized by deviant behavior, psychosomatic symptoms, and a feeling of marginality. Berry (1976) found that Native American groups experience high stress when the traditional culture is less similar to the second or mainstream culture. Groups experience lower stress when the culture is more similar to the second culture and has greater contact with other cultural groups.

Since students who consistently demonstrate heightened anxiety or stress, confused locus of

13

control, or lack of response are often referred for special services, it is imperative that teachers working with minority students who are experiencing acculturation consider the psychological "side-effects" of acculturation in assessment and programming. Appropriate placement for these students may be in cross-cultural counseling or acculturation assistance programs rather than in a special education program.

Studies of the effect of acculturation upon individuals have looked at the various steps involved and the degree of "culture shock" experienced (Adler, 1975; Juffer, 1983). Major variables which affect acculturation include the amount of time spent in the process, the quantity and quality of interaction, ethnicity or nation of origin, and language proficiency. These variables are discussed in detail in this section as they are especially relevant to assessment for placement in special education and form the basis of the acculturation screening device, Acculturation Quick Screen, which is recommended for the assessment of culturally and linguistically different learners.

The relationship between degree of acculturation and length of time (a) in school and (b) in orientation to the acculturation experience was explored in a study by Juffer (1983). She found that the length of time in school and receiving orientation both are highly correlated with degree of adaptation (acculturation). Juffer's findings of fewer problems in school cross-cultural social settings among more highly acculturated students are reflected by Finn (1982). He found that there were fewer referrals of culturally and linguistically different learners to special education in districts with bilingual programs. In addition, Szapocznik and Kurtines (1980) demonstrated that as bilingualism or biculturalism increased, socioemotional problems decreased. A study by Albino-Cordero (1981) showed that minority students in bilingual programs had fewer behavior problems than minority students in regular education programs.

14

The Szapocznik and Kurtines (1980) study focused on the importance of strong language skills in both the first language (Ll) and the second language (L2) as factors in mental health among minority subjects. The importance of English language proficiency in determining degree of and success in acculturation was documented by Juffer (1983). English ability was significant in three of four subcategories and in predicting a high composite score on the adaptation inventory. Some of the research in bilingual education also indicates the importance of proficiency in the native language as a foundation for proficiency in L2 acquisition and development, especially in the acculturation context (Skutnabb-Kangas & Toukamaa, 1976; Wells, 1981). Cummins (1986) provides an extensive description of the relationship between Ll and L2 development and stresses the vital importance of Ll in promoting educational success and cognitive development in the minority student in a cross-cultural learning situation. In his discussion of the psychological changes inherent in acculturation, Berry (1980) includes language and the types of adaptive changes which occur in both Ll and L2 as the two come into contact. Language ability has also been identified as one of the most important elements in making referral decisions (Knoff, 1983).

National origin or ethnicity has been examined as a factor in school achievement and referral to special education (Argulewicz & Elliott, 1981). Studies have shown a significant relationship between membership in an ethnic minority group and likelihood of being referred to special education. In addition, Juffer (1983) identified national origin as a factor which significantly predicted adaptation to a second culture.

Another factor which Juffer (1983) identified as significant in acculturation was the amount of interaction with mainstream American students. This may be interpreted as a function of the minority enrollment in the school. Finn (1982) indicates that there is a distinct relationship between minority school enrollment and special education referral and placement. As minority enrollment in a school district increases, the referral and placement of culturally and linguistically different students to special education becomes more consistent with mainstream referral rates (Collier, 1985; Finn, 1982).

Sociolinguistic Development

A further basic element of special concern in the assessment of minority students is language acquisition and development. Language is the primary medium through which culture and experiences are shared and transmitted from generation to generation and is a primary element in the acculturation of minority students. Language occurs within a social and interactive communicative context; the term "sociolinguistic development" is used to describe the comprehensiveness of language development and usage. It is important to identify and assess the minority student's sociolinguistic abilities in both first and second language since misunderstandings about sociolinguistic abilities frequently are involved in referrals of minority students to special education. The major sociolinguistic question is whether the student is linguistically different or linguistically disabled (lacking sociolinguistic abilities).

Understanding the process of sociolinguistic development is an attempt to resolve this question. Many minority students who are referred to special education are described as deficient in or lacking sociolinguistic skills entirely. This usually means that the student appears to have deficits in both English and the native language. There is ample evidence that the development of language skills for communication within a social context is a natural process and that human beings are genetically programmed for sociolinguistic acquisition (Chomsky, 1971; Lenneberg, 1967; Slobin, 1979; Snow, 1984). Therefore, a student who is "lacking language"

16

(Grosjean, 1982) would indeed be severely and unusually handicapped. Research has shown, however, that many minority students have well-established sociolinguistic systems in their first language as well as somewhat in English, but they use these systems selectively and nonacademically (Commins, 1986). Commins collected extensive natural language samples outside the school environment and concluded that minority students may well have sociolinguistic competence in both languages, but that their limited sociolinguistic performance in the academic setting obscures this underlying competence.

Slobin (1979) has shown that all students progress through several stages of language development (e.g., able to use two-word communications by about age 2). From 2 years of age, all children begin to incorporate the unique structures of their home language. Even moderately handicapped learners manage to acquire language. Only the most profoundly physically or mentally handicapped students who are subjected to extreme sensory deprivation or isolation fail to acquire language of some sort (Curtiss, 1982). Curtiss cites the case of a child, raised in complete isolation from human interaction, who learned limited but meaningful verbal communication after exposure to spoken language. All students, with few exceptions, learn a home language. Any student who can speak is not "lacking language," a disability often ascribed to bilingual students with limited English proficiency (Grosjean, 1982). "A normal child can learn any language to which he has adequate exposure" (Saville-Troike, 1983, p. 165).

Wells (1981) has demonstrated that the quality and quantity of verbal interaction students receive in the home language, whichever language is used, is the greatest predictor of later academic success in English. Cummins (1986) also cites research which supports the importance of quality first language development as a precursor to acquisition of English as a second language and later academic success. Those culturally and linguistically different learners who have not received "quality" development in their native language, and who have both poor first and second language proficiency, will need additional language development assistance based upon their sociolinguistic proficiency. This sometimes happens in non-English speaking homes where well-intentioned parents have insisted that children use only English when they, themselves, are unable to provide adequate interaction models. By doing so, they deny or discourage any use of the more dominant native language. Chesarek (1981) discusses this in regard to Native American students who have had continuing problems with academic achievement and second language acquisition even though their language ability in English is better than or equal to their ability in the native language.

Even these limited English or limited native language students have language, however, and they display sociolinguistic proficiency in a variety of nonacademic communicative settings (Commins, 1986). In conclusion, students from non-English speaking homes do not lack "language;" they may have an extensive sociolinguistic base which needs to be assessed as a basis for meaningful instruction in first language development, second language acquisition, and academic subject area instruction.

It is still not unusual to have students who are non-English speakers with proficiency in another language referred for assessment because of language disabilities. Rueda and Mercer (1985) noted that speech therapists were involved regularly in staffing of limited English speaking students while specialists in language difference (e.g., bilingual/ESL educators) were almost never involved. The identification of minority students as language disabled when they exhibit auditory perception and expressive problems in English conflicts with the provisions of P. L. 94-142 and other legislation and litigation. Only if minority students demonstrate receptive and expressive language problems both in their native language and in English can they be said to have a linguistic disability (Baca & Cervantes, in press). Thus, both English and native sociolinguistic development must be evaluated during the assessment process. Another sociocultural element to be addressed during assessment is that of differences in cognitive learning styles.

Cognitive Learning Styles

Cognition is the process of perceiving, attending, thinking, remembering, and knowing (Blumenthal, 1977). It is a continuous process which begins before birth and continues throughout life. Some people have more cognitive capacities than others, and some do not use what they possess. Education can affect the ability to develop and use cognitive processes. As Epstein (1978) notes, education can physically alter the brain, increasing the number of dendritic connections and the level of neural activity. There have been several studies of differences in cognitive style. Many researchers agree that the differences in how we conceptually organize our environment result in characteristic ways of learning from our experiences (Gardner, Jackson, & Messick, 1960; Mann & Sabatino, 1985; Ramirez & Castaneda, 1974).

Keogh (1973) defined cognitive style as the stable, typical, and consistent way in which individuals select and organize environmental data. Learning styles are the characteristic ways in which individual students respond to the instructional environment. While viewed as a consistent pattern of behavior, learning style has been shown to change with age and experience, especially exposure to cognitive and learning strategies (Stone & Wertsch, 1984).

Culture is the concept of things that a particular people use as models for perceiving, relating, and interpreting their environment. Cognitive development and cognitive learning style depend largely on the minority student's cultural background and experience (Collier & Hoover, 1987).

19

The culture shapes and influences the minority student's cognitive learning style; identifying these styles becomes an instructionally meaningful part of the assessment of minority students. Identifying the cognitive learning styles of the minority student contributes directly to the development of appropriate prereferral interventions and individualized education plans (see Section III).

Cognitive learning styles are the characteristic ways in which individual students respond to the learning task and instructional environment. They include (a) preference for analytic versus global interpretations, (b) broad versus narrow categorizations, (c) tolerance versus intolerance for ambiguous or unusual stimuli, (d) reflective versus impulsive tempo, (e) external versus internal locus of control, and (f) other characteristic learning patterns (Collier & Hoover, 1987). The reader is referred to Collier and Hoover (1987) and Mann and Sabatino (1985) for a detailed discussion on the identification of cognitive learning styles.

In conclusion, in addition to identifying the range of academic and behavior performance for students with learning and behavior problems, the key sociocultural factors to be identified during the assessment of minority students include (a) cultural and linguistic background, (b) experiential background, (c) the stage and pattern of acculturation, (d) patterns of sociolinguistic development, and (e) cognitive learning styles. Information about these sociocultural factors is available through a comprehensive review of existing student records, interviews, and observations, by testing, work sampling, and analytic teaching. These assessment techniques will be discussed in Section II. The nonclinical assessment of language proficiency is a special area in and of itself. The reader should consult Baca and Cervantes (in press), Butler, Bernstein, and Seidenberg (1988), Cummins (1984), Hammill (1987), and Omark and Watson (1984) for information about this topic.

Points for Discussion - Section I

1. Identify two factors associated with minority students which may be related to a teacher's referring a student unnecessarily for special education assessment.

2. Cite four aspects of a student's behavior or appearance which might bias a teacher's or psychologist's attitude toward the student.

3. Describe the concept of culture and relate this to cognition.

4. What is the relationship between culture and language?

5. Outline the requirements of P.L. 94-142 as they relate to the educational assessment of minority students.

SECTION II

ASSESSMENT TECHNIQUES FOR THE CULTURALLY AND LINGUISTICALLY DIFFERENT STUDENT

Information discussed in this section includes
several assessment techniques, with emphasis on
specific adaptations needed to develop meaningful
instructional information for minority students. The
discussion covers as part of assessment the
collection of information from existing records,
interviews, observations, testing, work sampling,
and analytic teaching. Although mention is made of
technical assessment procedures and theories, the
emphasis remains on gathering instructionally
meaningful information and the adaptation of
assessment techniques to address the special
sociocultural backgrounds of minority students. The
assessing of sociocultural factors which contribute
to learning and behavior problems in different
academic or socioemotional areas receives special
attention. The reader is referred to Salvia and
Ysseldyke (1988), Hammill (1987), Hammill, Brown,
and Bryant (1987), Gronlund (1985), and the American
Psychological Association (1985) for more
information about the assessment of learning and
behavior problems that are specific to subject areas
or social/emotional development.

Reviewing Existing Records

A complete review of various student school
records--official course grades, scores, and
anecdotal-records--can provide useful information
about the student, particularly in regard to
instructional history. Unfortunately, these records
are not always comprehensive, consistent, or even
organized meaningfully. Grades and scores are not
meaningful because they must be interpreted in light
of other information about the student which may not
be available. Also, anecdotal records may vary in
subjectivity depending on the experience,
background, knowledge, and training of the person
who wrote the report.

As with the other assessment techniques, it is
important to have specific assessment questions in
mind rather than approaching the task in a random,

haphazard manner. Clear assessment questions about the student's learning and behavior problems which need to be addressed are a prerequisite to the examination of school records. When these questions cannot be answered adequately by available records, the teacher will have a better idea about additional information that needs to be obtained. Wiederholt, Hammill, and Brown (1983) suggest questions to ask about the information in school records. These may be summarized as follows: (a) Is the information current? (b) Is it reliable? (c) Are there any discrepancies in the information? (d) Are there consistent patterns across the available information? Other related questions are: (a) How familiar was the person who completed the report with the student's culture and language? (b) Was the student's language proficiency assessed in both languages and how recent was the assessment?

A review of existing records is an appropriate initial action for concerned professionals when assessing minority students and should be designed to answer a comprehensive set of questions. Information essential to planning further assessment and instruction of minority students may be found in these records. Table 1 includes several questions related to sociocultural factors that should be considered in the assessment of minority students. Several of these questions are particularly important and will be discussed in detail.

One of the most important factors to consider before proceeding with the assessment process is the student's cultural and linguistic background. This is fundamental to all other elements of the assessment process, and it is a prerequisite for ascertaining language proficiency and level of acculturation. For example, a teacher may think that Maria is Hispanic because of her name and physical appearance. However, an examination of the records may reveal that she comes from a Central American Indian tribe in a rural area of Nicaragua. This information should raise several potential assessment concerns, including the language she

Table 1
Questions to be Answered through a Review
of Existing Records

1. What is the language(s) of the home?
2. What is the student's language proficiency in the home language? English language if different than home language?
3. What is the student's cultural background?
4. What are the child-rearing practices of the student's family culture?
5. How many years has the student been in the United States? Community? School?
6. What unusual trauma or stress has the student experienced in getting to the United States?
7. How well has the student adjusted to the mainstream culture?
8. How well has the student adjusted to the school culture?
9. What is the student's previous experiences with schooling?
10. How much time does the student spend in interacting with mainstream peers?
11. How much time does the student spend in interacting with cultural and linguistic peers?
12. What do the student's parents say about the student compared to his or her siblings?
13. What is the student's health and developmental history?
14. What is the student's response to previous instruction?
15. How well does the student perform in various instructional situations?
16. What is the student's response to ESL/Bilingual instruction?
17. How well does the student perform in various subject areas?
18. What changes in the student's performance have occurred over time (e.g., different subjects, schools, teachers)?
19. What are the student's academic and behavioral patterns in and out of the school setting?
20. What significant differences have been observed in the student's performance compared to his or her cultural and linguistic peers?
21. How well does the student see and hear?

speaks, the most dominant language in her home, whether she has been through physical or chemical warfare or has undergone unusual stress in her migration to the United States, her cultural background and the child rearing practices in her culture, and the reaction of her cultural group to acculturation situations in Nicaragua. If the anecdotal record contains nothing about the student's background, it is critical to obtain this information immediately. Siblings, parents, or other community members may be interviewed to collect this information.

Other important information to obtain from existing records is information which allows educators to make tentative decisions about the student's level of acculturation. This information can be ascertained by examining (a) the student's length of time in the United States and in the current community, (b) the amount of interaction with cultural peers vis-a-vis mainstream peers, (c) ethnicity or national origin, and (d) language proficiency in both languages. The Acculturation Quick Screen (AQS), developed by the author, is a device for recording and interpreting information about a student's level of acculturation. It organizes relevant information which can be used to determine an approximate level of acculturation. It is discussed in detail later in this section.

Unless the student is completely new to the school system, information related to language screening should be in existing records. Sometimes only information regarding the student's English language proficiency is available. In school districts with bilingual or ESL education programs, there is usually a screening procedure to determine if the student needs bilingual or ESL instruction. In many school districts, this instrument is the Language Assessment Scales (LAS) (DeAvila & Duncan, 1986). The LAS is available in English and Spanish; some districts have translated the instrument into other languages. However, a particular minority student may have been assessed with the LAS or another language screening instrument in English only. As discussed in Section I, it is crucial to instructional planning to identify the student's non-English language abilities. Therefore, the examiner needs to examine the existing records for evidence of the student's other sociolinguistic abilities. If this information does not exist, it must be determined through other assessment techniques, including the interview process.

Interviews

As with any assessment technique, it is important to have a clear purpose before proceeding with the interview to gather assessment information. The teacher and other professionals conducting the interview must understand clearly what information is to be ascertained, how it should be obtained, and why it is needed. In addition, the interviewer should record the information unobtrusively and should have a plan for dealing with any unusual reactions or answers. Teachers, parents, students, social workers, nurses, and paraprofessionals may be involved in the interview process. Indeed, varying the participants in the structured interview may result in more meaningful information related to the student's instructional needs. It is also important to vary the location and format of the interview, especially when any of the participants are not from the mainstream culture or have limited English proficiency.

Interviews can be very useful assessment techniques for examining the needs of culturally and linguistically different students. Their effectiveness, however, depends upon the skill of the person who conducts the interview. The interviewer must be familiar with the cultural and linguistic background of the student in order to determine whether a student's behaviors are culturally or linguistically appropriate. If the interviewer is fluent in the student's and parents' native language, these interviews will be more informative and meaningful for subsequent instruction. However, this is not always possible, especially when working with those who speak neither English nor Spanish. Interpreters may facilitate the interview process. In addition, it is important that the interviewer be sensitive to the nuances of cross-cultural communication and interaction. A more detailed discussion of the utilization and preparation of interpreters appears in Section III.

Some school districts employ special bilingual community liaison personnel to make home visits and to conduct interviews with non-English speaking parents. This approach can facilitate the collection of assessment information; however, it is important that the liaison be trained thoroughly in the techniques and rationale for obtaining information unobtrusively and in a manner that is culturally appropriate. If the interview is not conducted in an appropriate and comprehensive manner, the result may be information of little instructional value and the possible alienation of the family. The results of cross-cultural interviews (if they are conducted appropriately) can provide meaningful information such as (a) parents' perceptions about the student's behavior, developmental history, and upbringing; (b) family perception and treatment of the student in the home; and (c) the parents' perception of the source of the student's learning and behavior problems (Hammill, 1987).

The basic elements for cross-cultural interviews or verbal exchanges include (a) nonverbal reflection, (b) verbal reflection, and (c) cultural comfort zone. <u>Nonverbal reflection</u> refers to the interviewing technique of adjusting to the body language and gestures of the person who is being interviewed, though it should not be a mirror copy or obvious imitation. For example, if the person addressed is seated in a particular manner, the interviewer should assume a similar position. If the person interviewed uses many hand gestures, the interviewer should also use hand gestures. If the person addressed avoids eye contact as a sign of respect, the interviewer should try to decrease eye contact.

Verbal reflection refers to adapting one's tone of voice, intonation, latency, and rate of speech to that of the person who is addressed. For example, if the respondent speaks slowly and deliberately, the interviewer should avoid using rapid, excited speech. Tone, intonation, latency, and rate of speech convey different meanings in different cultures. Therefore, an interviewer should listen carefully to the patterns used by the respondent and should reflect them as much as possible.

Latency refers to the amount of time between the utterances of one person and those of another and can convey different meanings in different cultures. Spanish and English speakers tend to have rather short latency periods under certain circumstances (particularly during an argument or other excited exchange). American Indian cultures tend to equate latency with degree of respect and may have long pauses between one person's comment and another's response. In such a situation, an interviewer who asks a question and then asks another immediately after the response indicates little or no respect for the person's answer.

Cultural comfort zone refers to the awareness of one's own culture and sensitivity to the culture of the other person in the conversation. Awareness of one's cultural comfort zone includes not sitting or standing too close or too far away from the other person, not touching the person to whom one is speaking unless it is appropriate, responding to any signs of discomfort on the part of the respondent, and asking for clarification regarding the other person's discomfort or how to improve the situation. Table 2 provides an outline of a cross-cultural interview. The interviewer followed the question outline, providing probes as necessary, and allowed the respondent plenty of time to respond. As shown in the sample interview, the interviewer is gathering information from Juan's parent about Juan's cultural and linguistic background, previous

Table 2
Cross-Cultural Interview

1. How long have you and your family lived in this community? Tell me about how you came to live in this community.

    Probe: Did you come here because of job/family/other?
    Probe: How did you decide to move from where you lived before?

2. How has Juan adjusted to living in this community?
    Probe: What problems has he had with the move from _____?
    Probe: How does he feel about leaving your previous home?
    Probe: What does he miss about his previous home/community?
    Probe: What does he enjoy about this new community?
    Probe: How does he compare to your other children in adjustment?

3. Tell me about Juan's friends.
    Probe: Does Juan play with children in this neighborhood?
    Probe: What are they like compared to Juan?
    Probe: What languages do they speak while playing?
    Probe: With whom does Juan spend the most time? Tell me about them. How do they compare to your other children's playmates?

4. What languages do you speak at home?

    Probe: What language do you use during dinner?
    How do you decide what language to use?

5. Tell me about Juan's previous school experiences.

    Probe: Did Juan like being in school before?
    Probe: How did he do? What were his favorite subjects?
    Probe: Tell me about Juan's attendance.

6. Tell me what you think would help Juan be successful in school.

    Probe: When Juan does something you like, what do you do?
    Probe: When you want to teach Juan how to do something, what do you do?

7. Tell me about Juan's early childhood development.

    Probe: How does he compare to your other children?

school experience, sociolinguistic development, and learning style. The interviewer is also gathering information which will assist in determining Juan's level of acculturation and degree of adjustment to American culture and society in addition to his response to the culture and environment of the school.

The information from this interview would be used to supplement the information gathered from a review of existing records in an attempt to estimate Juan's level of acculturation and to identify the cultural and sociolinguistic factors which must be addressed in greater detail during the assessment process. The information collected about Juan's experience with and response to the school environment and learning style can be used immediately by the classroom teacher in modifying Juan's instructional plan. An observation of his response to these modifications would then be appropriate, especially as related to earlier observations.

Observations

A clear understanding of concerns about the student's behavior or performance is a prerequisite to effective observation. As in the interview technique, it is helpful to have predetermined questions that are to be answered as a means of analyzing the results of the observation, although there are situations when this information may bias the observation. In some circumstances, it is better to observe the student's interactions and behaviors without reference to prior information regarding the teacher's concern. In any observation, however, what is seen as noteworthy is highly subjective; the background, training, and preparation of the observer becomes a significant factor in the accuracy and usefulness of the observation.

Observation can be an appropriate assessment technique for examining the needs of culturally and linguistically diverse students. It is highly dependent upon the skill of the examiner who must be familiar with the cultural and linguistic background of the student. When observing student behavior, the observer should know what is culturally or linguistically appropriate for that particular student.

There are also cultural pitfalls which must be avoided when making observations. A structured observation can provide instructionally meaningful information because it is the one assessment technique which permits evaluation within a natural environment. Just as the nature of the student's culture and the nature of school culture are a part of that natural environment, the observer must exercise caution when interpreting observational data. For example, a Navajo student may be observed looking at the floor every time the teacher speaks to him. If the observer knows that this behavior is culturally appropriate as a sign of respect and attention, the act of looking at the floor will not be misinterpreted as an indication of disrespect, defiance, low self-esteem or inattention. If an observer sees an Eskimo girl looking surprised (e.g., raising her eyebrows) when the teacher asks her a question, he might think she did not know the answer, or that she was not familiar with what had been asked. However, an observer familiar with the Eskimo culture knows that raising one's eyebrows is a way of giving a positive response (i.e., saying 'yes'). In many cases, it may be difficult to employ an observer from the same cultural and linguistic background as the student. However, the successful use of this technique requires that the observer be someone who is sensitive to and knowledgeable about the student's culture. In addition, a videotape of the student's behavior in the classroom or playground environment may serve as a basis for discussion by a multidisciplinary cross-cultural team who can address the student's behavior from a variety of perspectives. Table 3 provides a guide for cross-cultural observations. The guide has been completed for illustrative purposes.

Table 3
Example: Cross-Cultural Observation

Student: Ba Vang   Grade: 3rd
Teacher: Ms. Hartley   Observer: Ms. Homer
Date: 10/8   Time of day: Morning

Length of observation: 45 minutes

Environment: There were 20 students seated at separate desks placed in clusters around the room. There are several learning centers in the room and the students have decorated the room with materials and pictures appropriate to harvest celebrations.

Activity: Students were working independently at their desks while Ms. Hartley had a group of six students including Ba gathered around a table in the 'science center' with a number of globes representing star positions and planets as well as an ephemeris of the current night sky. After positioning the globes, the students returned to their seats to work on a drawing and worksheet about the night sky while another small group came into the science area.

Content: Ms. Hartley asked the students to look at the ephemeris and then use the models of planets and moon to represent where these would be in relation to Earth that night. This was part of their regular 3rd grade science lesson on the Solar System.

Strategies: Ms. Hartley was very positive and supportive using praise and touch to reinforce the students' achievements with the lesson. She had also reviewed the names of the globes and their location on the ephemeris before having the students construct the model.

Setting: This small group was located in the room's science center away from the other students and partially screened from them. All of the students were standing around the table which held the globes.

Observed behavior: Ba said, "Ms. Hartley, it is a lot of ball." Ba looked at the globes and touched them, but soon his attention seemed to wander and he started trying to get the attention of his cousin in the other section of the room. When Ms. Hartley called his name and asked him to move one of the globes into position, he looked at her and the globes, but did not touch the correct one. He smiled and shrugged. One of the other students asked Ms. Hartley if he could move the globe, as he knew which one and where to place it in relation to the Earth globe. Ms. Hartley asked the student to assist Ba in moving the globe. The student took one of Ba's hands and placed it on the correct globe, then both moved the globe into place. When Ms. Hartley asked the student why he had not just told Ba where the globe went, he replied that Ba did not understand him very well. Ba did not speak during this lesson, although he did go over to his cousin after the activity and talk to him in Hmong before the cousin went over to participate in the science activity. When Ba was in his seat, he held his pencil and looked at his worksheet, then got up and looked over the partition at his cousin in the science center. When his cousin came out after the completion of the globe activity, he spoke to Ba and motioned him back to his seat. Ba returned to his seat and began to draw small circles on the paper and then colored the space around the circles black.

Summary: Ba has not been in this country very long and is evidently unfamiliar with globes and other representations of the objects in the sky. He uses English in BICS, but did not respond to the teacher's directions in English. He appeared to grasp the general idea of what needed to be done on the worksheet, but still could not associate his own drawing of a nighttime sky to that which was required. He appeared curious about the lesson and wanted to know more. He may never have seen symbols and models of sky objects before. His performance improved whenever someone gave him concrete or physical examples and guidance.

The observation in Table 3 focuses on several particular concerns. It provides information about Ba's response to the learning environment in the classroom as well as information about his experiential background, cultural and sociolinguistic development, and learning style. The key elements of the observation are (a) an adequate length of time; (b) an activity which provides comprehensive information about the student's performance; (c) a clear understanding of the content, strategies, and setting of the activity; and (d) a comprehensive description of the observed behavior. The information from the observation, together with information from existing records and previous interviews of the student's parents, enable the observer to draw several conclusions about the student's cultural and background experience, sociolinguistic development, and cognitive learning style. For example, the observer concluded that Ba had basic interpersonal communication skills in English but limited use of cognitive academic language proficiency in English and in Hmong, and, that Ba responded well when given concrete examples and demonstrations. An additional element of the observation was an examination of the student's work sample, in this case the worksheet of the night sky, produced during the observation.

Work Samples

Analysis of students' work samples is a very meaningful assessment technique for instructional purposes. Samples of student work or production may be collected for any subject or content area as well as students' speech, language, and fine or gross motor performance. Samples may be examined directly in a variety of instructional situations. The analysis of work samples may be informal (e.g., noting the presence or absence of various letters or shapes) or formal (e.g., more systematic analyses such as the Reading Miscue Inventory, Goodman & Burke, 1972, or Formal Reading Inventory,

Wiederholt, 1985).

As with other assessment techniques, knowledge of the student's presenting problem and concomitant assessment questions are essential elements of this technique. Work samples can be highly structured or informal depending upon the teacher's needs and circumstances. However, familiarity with and sensitivity to the student's cultural and linguistic background are crucial. For example, if the teacher collects examples of the student's writing and notes that it shows peculiarities in shape and directionality, the teacher should determine the kind of orthography the student used in the native language. The student's use of orthographic characteristics from the native language may continue to pose problems when writing English.

However, it is instructionally meaningful for the teacher to know that this problem is due to a learned behavior and not to a possible perceptual problem. The correct instructional response, then, is to assist the student in transferring and transforming orthographic skills into a more appropriate format. Another example of cross-cultural differences in work samples might be seen in the syntax the student uses in language arts activities. For example, rather than write, "A chair is something that is used in a house," a German student might write, "A chair is something what is used in a house," because of differences between vas and das in German. A Navajo student may write or say "Nell my name" rather than "Nell is my name," as this is the direct translation from Navajo. Also a Navajo may say "Man how called?" which is a direct translation of "What is that man's name?" in Navajo. In Czechoslovakia, people do not say "The boy is in the sun." Rather, the expression is, "The boy is on the sun." These and other linguistic differences between English and other languages may pose considerable problems for minority students in written and spoken classroom work.

Different performance seen on students' work samples may also be due to different instructional experiences. For example, a teacher referred a student to a child study team because of consistent and recurring poor performance in spelling even though this student, who was Hispanic, spoke English as well as her peers. An examination of spelling work samples revealed substitutions such as "through" for "tough," but words such as "rough" and "tongue" were never substituted for "tough." A thorough analysis of work samples led to the conclusion, verified later by a call to her previous school, that she had been in a spelling program which emphasized the use of configuration (i.e., the shape of words) as a strategy. In addition, a search of her health history indicated that she needed glasses, but had not had a new prescription in years. This student could not see clearly enough to distinguish individual letters and was using the configuration strategy to approximate the correct spelling.

If the teacher is not familiar with the student's cultural and linguistic background, student work samples should be examined with the assistance of someone who is sensitive to the student's background. This is a situation where a teacher assistance child intervention team may be helpful. The concerned teacher could share work samples with the team members and a group discussion may lead to a more comprehensive evaluation of the student's performance. Additional questions about the student's work may be raised and a plan developed for collecting further work samples. Teachers must be aware of linguistic and cultural substitutions or modifications and the possible lack of familiarity with the task or terminology required. These two areas, familiarity and transfer, may influence the student's work samples in any curriculum area.

Testing

Tests can be defined as any situations in which a student is presented with a set of tasks or questions intended to elicit specific behavior which can provide psychometric scores (American Psychological Association, 1985). They are considered the most objective means of assessment, a status which appears to give them more validity than other assessment techniques. Unfortunately, although aware of the cultural and linguistic bias inherent in tests, most professionals see test scores as "true" measures of students' achievement and performance and often accept test scores as the sole basis for determining the instructional needs of students.

All assessment techniques are classified according to their degree of standardization. Tests which have acceptable reliability and validity are viewed as formal tests whereas those with little or no evidence of standardization are considered informal tests. Hammill (1987) discusses the advantage of utilizing formal as well as informal assessment techniques when measuring students' achievement and performance.

Hammill points out that although formal tests may be technically reliable and valid, they often provide limited information of little instructional use due to the test setting and the restrictive procedures that must be followed during their administration. Informal assessment, he indicates, can be used effectively (a) to diagnose and plan for the resolution of instructional problems, (b) to ascertain the extent of students' knowledge of a particular subject, and (c) to assess achievement and performance in areas not addressed by formal tests which are currently available.

Reference of Interpretation

In addition to the degree of standardization, tests are also classified according to how scores are interpreted. Formal and informal assessment techniques can be interpreted in a norm-, criterion- or nonreferenced manner. In norm-referenced tests, student scores are based on a comparison of test scores with a hypothetically average score which is derived by statistically determining the average score of a representative group with common characteristics. Such a comparison is often problematic for minority students because they may not have been included in the representative group that was used to norm the test. This is especially true with nationally normed tests. It is more instructionally meaningful to determine local norms for a particular test, thereby including the minority population in the norming process. Further discussion on establishing local norms is found in Omark and Watson (1984) and Elliott and Bretzing (1980).

Criterion-referenced interpretation compares student scores on a test to a predetermined level of performance. According to Salvia and Ysseldyke (1988), criterion-referenced assessment provides answers to specific performance questions. For example, criterion-referenced assessment clearly provides the answer to "Does the student spell 'gato' correctly?" Norm-referenced assessment would compare the spelling performance to the performance of the student's peers. Clearly, the use of criterion-referenced assessment is more meaningful for instructional purposes. It can identify and monitor instructional needs and can place students in a particular curricular sequence. Although criterion-referenced assessment is less culturally and linguistically biased than norm-referenced assessment, the practitioner must consider the sociocultural factors that were discussed in Section I.

Nonreferenced interpretation uses test performance to identify student strategies in problem solving. It is especially meaningful when assessing minority students who are culturally and linguistically different because it takes into account their cognitive learning styles, which often differ from those of the mainstream population. More effective learning strategies can be taught if the teacher is aware of how students reach erroneous conclusions or how they reach acceptable conclusions in an inefficient way (Hammill, 1987).

Formal Assessment

Standards for educational and psychological testing (American Psychological Association, 1985) describes a test as valid only if there is evidence that test scores provide legitimate information for an intended use. This is not often evidenced in measures of school ability, particularly in the standardized intelligence tests, used to guide the delivery of effective instruction for minority students with learning and behavior problems. The latest revision of Standards contains a new section, Testing of linguistic minorities, which reflects an increased sensitivity to these concerns.

It is important to remember that every test administered in English to a non-native English speaker becomes, in large part, a language test. It may not in fact measure what it is intended to measure. Tests of aptitude and achievement administered to language minority students are intended to assess skills and competencies, not English proficiency. Attention should be given to the assessment of the student's range of communicative competence in English across naturalistic settings in addition to obtaining information about a student's problem solving competencies in specific skill areas via an array of assessment instruments and devices.

Sociocultural norms for appropriate language behavior may affect the student's verbal fluency and rate of production. This is of special concern to test administrators who attempt to elicit evidence of competency in a particular skill area. The person who administers the test must be "functionally familiar" (Duran, in preparation) with the student's communication style and communicative repertoire. Functional familiarity goes beyond sensitivity to the standard literate use of the native language. It requires that the test administrator sense how

41

students can be helped to maximize their communication knowledge as they respond to test questions (Duran, in preparation). A more detailed discussion of the strengths and weaknesses of specific tests commonly administered to minority students as part of special education assessment is found in Cummins (1984), Figueroa (1986), and Ortiz and Yates (1984). The major underlying problem with formal assessment of minority students for special education purposes is the lack of adequate connection between assessment outcomes and the subsequent instruction that is provided as a result of special education classification (Heller, Holtzman, & Messick, 1982).

The two most controversial issues in the formal assessment of minority students are standardization and norming. According to Hammill (1987), standardization is applicable to all assessment techniques and a knowledge of reliability and validity is important when interpreting data collected from any assessment technique (e.g., analytic teaching, interviews, observations, testing). Hammill notes that, while norms are often associated with standardized devices, their presence is by no means an essential element of standardization; in many cases norms are superfluous. This is important to remember when interpreting the test scores of culturally and linguistically different students. With precise and consistent administrative procedures, testing and other assessment techniques adapted for use with culturally and linguistically different students can yield reliable, valid results and can be interpreted in a consistent manner without being norm-referenced.

One way to adapt tests for minority students is to evaluate the instruments for content and language bias. Bias occurs for several reasons: experiential background, socioeconomic status, family history, cultural background and sociolinguistic background, sex, and other variables. For example, a student may know that in a test picture the pig is missing a

curl in his tail. However, the student may not know
that a cheviot is a type of sheep or that a picture
of a saucer is to be matched with a teacup. The
student might be judged as having an ability deficit
while in reality test performance merely exhibits
differences in experience background.

Adaptation to correct for content and language
bias necessitates an evaluation of cultural and
linguistic appropriateness in the most recent
edition of the test and in the student's native
language, if available. The first and perhaps the
simplest step in adaptation is to conduct a visual
and structural overview of the illustrations in a
test to determine if they are within the student's
experiential background. It is also very important
to identify the validity and reliability data as
well as the standardization data to determine the
representativeness of the population sample. This
information is very useful in the adaptation process
because it provides insight into the structure of
the test under consideration. For example, many
tests are constructed so that items become
increasingly more difficult. The scoring and
interpretation of such tests are based on the
progression of item difficulty which was normed with
a population that may not have included students of
diverse linguistic and cultural backgrounds. These
tests, then, are not totally appropriate for
culturally and linguistically different students.

Tests which use geometric patterns and no written
language also illustrate this inappropriateness. The
patterns become increasingly more complicated and
asymmetrical. When a student misses several
consecutive items, it is assumed that a ceiling
level has been reached and that testing should be
discontinued. Yet studies show that Crow students do
better on the last portion of the test than on the
beginning, "easier" portion. Chesarek (1981)
suggests that very often performance is related to
the cultural use of asymmetry, a concept that test
designers and administrators need to bear in mind
when culturally and linguistically different

learners are assessed. Cultural values reflected by the test items, therefore, must also be considered in the adaptation process. Unfamiliar or conflicting cultural values may influence the student's response and consequently may provide inaccurate information.

A general overview of illustrations and test structure should be followed by an evaluation of the response modes which the testing instrument requires. Are responses allowed in the student's most proficient means of communication, and do they reflect actual knowledge of the assessment objectives rather than a level of literacy or language proficiency? If the assessment concern is whether or not the non-English speaking student knows the multiplication facts or something about colors and light refraction, the test must actually measure this ability and not the student's English proficiency. The language of the test items should not prevent nor hinder the assessment of specific knowledge or ability.

Yet another consideration is whether the assessment information is instructionally meaningful for the student. Before using any assessment procedure or device, the teacher or examiner should have a clear picture of the information to be gathered and of its usefulness in improving the student's instructional program. If the instrument or procedure does not provide instructionally meaningful information, the examiner should have another specific purpose in mind for the assessment. It is not appropriate to assess without a specific purpose, even when an assessment of general ability is desired. General ability and aptitude testing is useful because it may identify students who need more structured and minutely sequenced learning. However, it would be more to the point to test for these needs directly. Most general aptitude and ability tests rely on a student's previous experience and exposure to mainstream cultural concepts, and therefore are of little educational use in assessing students from different cultural and linguistic backgrounds. Some instruments have been developed in different languages, such as the Woodcock Language Proficiency Battery (Woodcock, 1987), KeyMath Diagnostic Arithmetic Test (1976), and Diagnostic Inventory of Basic Skills (Brigance, 1978), or with less intrinsic experiential bias, such as the Kaufman Assessment Battery for Children (Kaufman, 1983), International Performance Scale (Leiter, 1976), and Learning Potential Assessment Device (Feuerstein, 1982), and may be useful within a given instructional context. However, we must not take tests at face value just because they have a tradition of use in assessments; specific purposes for their use should be determined prior to selection.

Informal Assessment

Informal assessment has three effective uses: to diagnose and plan for instructional problems, to probe the extent of the student's knowledge of a subject, and to assess areas for which formal tests are not available. Both formal and informal testing are important assessment techniques which can be interpreted in either a norm-, criterion- or nonreferenced manner for minority students. Informal assessment techniques such as record review, interview, observation, and work sample anlaysis show little or no evidence of standardization. Informal assessment is useful in the evaluation of student performance, and in the analysis of curriculum (including content, instructional strategies, instructional settings, and student behaviors) (Hoover, 1988). This type of assessment provides information about the student's current status, the task, the setting, and the efficacy of instructional strategies used. Teacher-made criterion-referenced tests are a common example of informal assessment. While formal tests include a broad range of items from a general curriculum area and use few test items to measure each specific skill, informal assessment devices focus on one or more subskills within a curricular area in an

Figure 1
AQS – A Guide to Estimating Level of Acculturation

NAME _____ Emiliano _____   SCHOOL _____ Smith Elementary _____

DATE OF BIRTH _____ 2-10-81 _____   SEX _____ M _____   GRADE _____ First _____

AGE AT ARRIVAL IN U.S. _____ 7 _____   LANGUAGE(s) SPOKEN AT HOME _____ Spanish/Quechua _____

	Raw data	AQS Scale Score
Number of years, United States	2 months	1
Number of years, School District	6 weeks	1
Number of years, ESL and/or bilingual education	0 years	1
LAU category	A	1
Native language proficiency	Least (Oral)	1
English language proficiency	Least	1
Ethnicity/nation of origin	Native American (Peru)	1
Percentage minority enrollment in attending school	85%	1
AQS Scale Score TOTAL		8

AQŜ SCALE SCORE GUIDELINES

Number of years, US/SD

Under 1	= 1
1 - 2	= 2
3 - 4	= 3
5 - 6	= 4
Over 6	= 5

Number of years, ESL/BE

0.0 - 1.0	= 1
1.1 - 1.5	= 2
1.6 - 2.0	= 3
2.1 - 2.5	= 4
2.6 - 3.0	= 5

LAU category

A	= 1
B	= 2
C	= 3
D	= 4
E	= 5

Ethnicity

Native American	= 1
Hispanic	= 2
Asian/Pac. Is.	= 3
Black/Mideast	= 4
White/European	= 5

Percentage enrollment

81% - 100%	= 1
61% - 80%	= 2
41% - 60%	= 3
21% - 40%	= 4
0% - 20%	= 5

Language proficiency

Least	= 1
proficient	= 2
	= 3
Most	= 4
proficient	= 5

attempt to provide a more comprehensive assessment (McLoughlin & Lewis, 1986). The Acculturation Quick Screen and the Curriculum–Based Assessment (CBA) procedures, discussed below, are specific examples of informal assessment.

The Acculturation Quick Screen (AQS) is a guide for the collection of information relevant to the student's level of acculturation, which is a necessary precursor to formal assessment. It is based on research into the effect of acculturation on referral and staffing decisions (Adler, 1975; Berry, 1980; Collier, 1985; Juffer, 1983), and is an initial screening instrument which provides an approximate measure of a student's level of acculturation into the mainstream American culture. It should be used only to guide further assessment and instructional planning. Not to be used in isolation nor as a predictive tool, the Acculturation Quick Screen provides useful supplemental information that may substantiate decisions for more intensive intervention.

The information to complete the AQS may be obtained from a review of records, interviews, and observation. Figure 1 illustrates the information that can be provided by the AQS. In this example, Emiliano's score of 8 is the lowest possible score on the AQS, indicating very little or no acculturation. If Emiliano was literate or highly proficient in his native language, his score would be 12. A very acculturated student might score 35 to 40 on the AQS. Students like Emiliano, who score at the lower end of the AQS, may benefit from peer counseling with others who are in the process of acculturation, instruction in cultural survival skills, specific cross-cultural communication strategies, and intensive assistance with linguistic and cultural transfer. They may also need intensive language development and second language acquisition assistance depending on the level of their first and second language skills.

Another example of informal assessment is the curriculum–based assessment(CBA) procedure which

48

measures school skills directly. The content of CBA is determined by the classroom curriculum. This type of procedure is obtrusive and requires that a test or a series of tasks be added to the instructional situation (McLoughlin & Lewis, 1986). CBAs are teacher-made tests designed to measure directly the students' skills at specified levels; they are criterion-referenced, and they are a powerful element of collaborative consultation among the regular classroom teacher and special educators at all stages of the assessment process. CBA is based on the assumption that a curricular area may be divided into discrete steps or facts and that learning itself consists of the mastery of discrete elements (McLoughlin & Lewis, 1986). If a student fails to answer a CBA test item correctly, the assumption is that remedial assistance is needed involving the unmastered skills and content of the CBA item. Idol, Nevin, and Paolucci-Whitcomb (1986) discuss CBA in great detail and provide many examples from different subject areas. They have identified several steps necessary when using CBA:

1. Sample items should be selected from the curriculum.

2. Items should be arranged in order of difficulty.

3. Selected items should be administered as a test to the whole class.

4. The test should be repeated at least two times with different items from the same content.

5. Assessment should be conducted across several curricular levels.

6. Student performance as a class should be recorded.

7. Acceptable levels of student performance or mastery which reflect the typical classroom

performance should be determined. This can be accomplished by normative sampling.

8. Curriculum-Based Assessment should be conducted with individual students or groups of students immediately prior to instruction on a topic.

9. Results should be studied to determine which students have already mastered the skills targeted for instruction, which students possess sufficient preskills to begin instruction, and which students lack mastery of preskills.

10. CBA should be readministered after instruction on the topic. Results should be analyzed to determine which students have mastered the skills and are ready to begin a new topic, which students are making sufficient progress but require more practice, and which students are making insufficient progress and require teacher modification of some aspect of instruction.

11. Instruction should be modified to reflect student performance (i.e., don't repeat mastered areas and provide more assistance in the unmastered areas).

12. CBA should be readministered periodically throughout the year to assess long-term retention.

As illustrated in these steps, the classroom teacher may develop CBA in any subject area with which minority students have particular difficulty (e.g., reading in English). The teacher selects sample vocabulary words and concepts from the reading materials that are used in the class and arranges them in order of difficulty, using the scope and sequence of the materials as a guide if need be. Some of these words and concepts are then administered as a test to the whole class. The teacher repeats this procedure using different items from the reading materials at various levels, and records the class performance. Acceptable levels of performance may be determined by appraising the average performance of the class and of reading groups within the class. The teacher may then administer the CBA to the minority students about whom there is particular concern. Depending upon student performance on the CBA, the teacher will modify the instructional setting, strategies, or content.

Practitioners using CBA procedures must have a clear understanding of what constitutes curriculum. Curriculum is the comprehensive environment of instruction including content, instructional strategies, instructional setting, and student behaviors (Hoover, 1988; Hoover & Collier, 1986). If only the content of instruction is used in CBA, it has limited value as a primary assessment technique for minority students.

Analytic Teaching

Analytic teaching, sometimes labeled diagnostic or prescriptive teaching, involves the observation of student behavior in the learning of particular tasks that have been subdivided into their constituent components. The teacher determines the tasks and components to be undertaken based on assessment questions concerning student abilities. For example, if the teacher is unsure of the student's ability to tell time, the student may be asked to perform a sequence of increasingly difficult tasks related to telling time: Count to 12; count by fives; give the definition of a clock; name its parts; explain their function; draw a 12-hour clock; draw a clock indicating 5-minute intervals; identify or draw various times.

During analytic teaching, it is important for the teacher to note what the student can and cannot do in regard to the task. In addition, cultural and linguistic differences should be noted and addressed by varying the sequence or nature of the analytic

Table 4
Steps in Analytic Teaching

1. Identify the current instructional condition or baseline performance.
2. Identify an activity which will assess the student's problem(s).
3. Identify the steps necessary to successfully complete the activity.
4. Construct a sequence and completion checklist based upon the steps.
5. Construct a self-analysis checklist based on this sequence for the student to complete.
6. Develop and implement an instructional activity which incorporates the steps and sequence to be assessed.
7. Observe the student during this activity, noting the results, and have the student complete his self-analysis.
8. Analyze the results obtained from the checklists.
9. Identify and select a new instructional strategy to evaluate.
10. Implement the new instructional strategy for a brief period.
11. Continue to regularly assess the student's performance.
12. Implement a second new instructional strategy if desired.
13. Continue to regularly assess the student's performance.
14. Plot the student's performance data for the baseline and the intervention phases on a graph. Compare performance across the interventions. (Steps 1-8 make-up the baseline phase and steps 10 and 12 are the two intervention phases) Only one element at a time should be changed in intervention. The instructional factor that produced change in the student's performance can then be identified.

tasks. Analytic teaching analyzes a student's behavior while he is engaged in ongoing instructional situations. The procedure is used to gather instructionally meaningful information which may be used to form hypotheses about the nature of the student's learning and behavior problems, in order to determine subsequent steps in assessment or instruction and to monitor student progress.

The steps involved in analytic teaching are illustrated in Table 4. They include (a) selection and identification of the activity, (b) task analysis (sequential performance steps) of the activity, (c) observation of the student while engaged in the activity, (d) noting the student's responses against some predetermined frame of reference, and (e) determination of the next stage of analysis based upon the results of the observed behavior. When implementing analytic teaching, it is important to change only one element at a time during the intervention activity. The instructional element that produces a change in the student's performance can then be identified.

The following description of a lesson in spelling is an example of how analytic teaching can be used to assess informally a student's cognitive learning style. The teacher first identifies an activity in which the student's success or failure is related to his approach to the learning task. Spelling words are selected and the steps the student needs to follow are outlined. The teacher works with the student to develop a self checklist. The steps suggested by the student to learn the new vocabulary may be: Repeat the words as the teacher says and spells them; say them four times; try to spell them correctly without looking; check the spelling and do more practice with those incorrectly spelled.

As the student follows these steps, the teacher observes the student's attempt to learn the new vocabulary and notes the results. The teacher might indicate to the student that the activities which depend on auditory cues may not produce the best results. The student is instructed to try a new

Table 5
Sociocultural Indicators

FACTORS	ASSESSMENT TECHNIQUES	SAMPLE INDICATORS OF SOCIOCULTURAL FACTORS CONTRIBUTING TO THE PROBLEM
Cultural and Linguistic Background	Review of Records	Comes from non-English speaking home Comes from a culture or ethnic group different from mainstream America Culture values support of family/group over individual effort Comes from non-English speaking geographic area Culturally appropriate behaviors different from mainstream America
Acculturation Level	Observation Records Interview Testing	Recent immigrant Doesn't interact much with mainstream peers or cultural group Displays heightened stress of anxiety in cross-cultural interactions Expresses or displays sense of isolation or alienation in cross-cultural interactions

Category	Assessment Methods	Descriptors
Experiential Background	Interview Records Testing Analytic Teaching Observation Work Samples	Migrant Limited or sporadic school Low socioeconomic status Little exposure to subject Not familiar with material No previous schooling Few appropriate cognitive learning strategies Few preskills Does not know how to behave in classroom Different terms/concepts for subject areas or materials and content Displays inappropriate survival skills
Sociolinguistic Development	Observation Testing Analytic Teaching Work Samples	Doesn't speak English Limited CALP in native language Limited BICS in English Rarely speaks in class Speaks only to cultural peers Limited CALP in English Asks peers for assistance in understanding Appears to know English but can't follow English directions in class
Cognitive and Learning Styles	Observation Analytic Teaching	Cognitive learning style differs from teacher's Cognitive learning strategies different or inappropriate in relation to teacher's teaching style Retains survival strategies which are no longer appropriate

approach to learning the vocabulary, such as using different rehearsal strategies. Writing the words as she says them, pausing to picture what the word means, and then writing the word down as the teacher says it out loud are rehearsal strategies that the student is encouraged to learn. The teacher then observes how the student performs with a new list of words; if student performance improves, that particular learning strategy is encouraged and promoted. If performance does not improve, other strategies such as analogy or kinesthetic cues are suggested. The teacher continues to assess the student's performance in these activities and to modify teaching technique if necessary. Analytic teaching is instructionally meaningful and is useful in all aspects of the curriculum, especially as a prereferral intervention activity. Interventions derived from analytic teaching assessment focus on the teaching of enabling skills, that is, subskills necessary to perform more complex behaviors.

This section concludes with an illustration of when each of these five assessment techniques may be used appropriately to assess cultural and linguistic factors in minority students. Table 5 provides this information. Table 5 lists the five cultural and linguistic factors discussed in Section I, followed by the identification of suggested primary assessment techniques to assess whether a suspected problem results, in part, from sociocultural factors. Also provided in the table are indicators which signal the presence of specific sociocultural factors which may be contributing to the student's learning and behavior problems. If there are few "red flags," sociocultural factors may not be a primary element in the students' learning and behavior problems. In this case, something other than language and culture factors (possibly a handicapping condition) is contributing to the minority student's problems with the learning environment. If many "red flags" exist, however, sociocultural factors may be influencing the student's performance.

Points for Discussion - Section II

1. Identify two sources of information about a student's functioning in educational settings.

2. What is the difference in the information obtained from norm-referenced, criterion-referenced, and non-referenced tests?

3. Identify four methods that provide useful information in a nonbiased assessment.

4. Define the term "norm" and list three norms against which a child might be evaluated other than national norms.

5. List three factors intrinsic to the student, and unrelated to intelligence, which might affect the outcome of a standardized test.

SECTION III

ASSESSMENT PROCESS FOR CULTURALLY AND LINGUISTICALLY DIFFERENT STUDENTS

This section describes the assessment process as it applies to culturally and linguistically different learners, including the three major elements of the assessment process: referral, staffing, and placement. The elements of the assessment process for minority students may be detailed as follows:

1. Referral: Screening to determine if sociocultural factors contribute to learning and behavioral problems, to identify learning and behavioral problems that are not due to sociocultural factors, to determine if the student responds to sociocultural interventions implemented during the referral stage (prereferral intervention), and to determine if the student requires additional screening and assessment (formal referral).

2. Staffing: Further screening and comprehensive assessment by a multidisciplinary team to determine conclusively the student's need for special assistance and the nature of the student's learning and behavior problems, and a multidisciplinary team meeting to determine the student's instructional needs.

3. Placement: Decision-making concerning whether or not the student is eligible for special education, and if so, development of a plan for program instruction and monitoring. If it is determined that the student requires special education services, appropriate placement is made into a special education program that meets the student's unique instructional needs, and an individual educational plan (IEP) is developed that outlines these needs and how they will be met, as well as a plan to monitor its effectiveness. If it is determined that the student does not need special education services, the student is usually returned to the general education program with suggestions for cultural and linguistic interventions in the general education classroom.

All three elements are included in the assessment process and are discussed in regard to culturally and linguistically diverse students who also have learning and behavior problems. The following discussion addresses the three elements of the assessment process as they apply to minority students. However, primary emphasis is on the prereferral process, since it has been identified as the critical key to appropriate assessment for minority students (California Department of Education, in press; Collier, 1987; Ortiz & Garcia, 1988).

Figure 2 illustrates the process of assessment for minority students. The three major elements of the assessment process--referral, staffing, and placement--form the setting in which assessment activities occur. The six assessment techniques described in Section II are used to address the five sociocultural factors which may contribute to and compound the student's learning and behavior problems. The purpose of assessing minority students according to this paradigm is to determine (a) whether or not sociocultural factors are major contributors to students' learning and behavior problems, and (b) whether sociocultural factors <u>and</u> the presence of handicapping conditions contribute to students' learning and behavior problems. When these variables impact the student's learning, it is essential to assess the student's academic and behavior functioning. For a concise discussion of the assessment of specific learning and behavior problems, the reader is directed to Salvia and Ysseldyke (1988), Hammill (1987), and McLoughlin and Lewis (1986).

The information obtained from all assessment procedures is used to develop the individualized instructional plan (IEP) documenting appropriate content, strategies, and classroom settings necessary to provide appropriate education. Monitoring the implementation of the IEP is conducted regularly and re-evaluated periodically. This process may lead to reassessment procedures and a recycling through the process as indicated in Figure 2.

Figure 2
Assessment Process for Minority Students

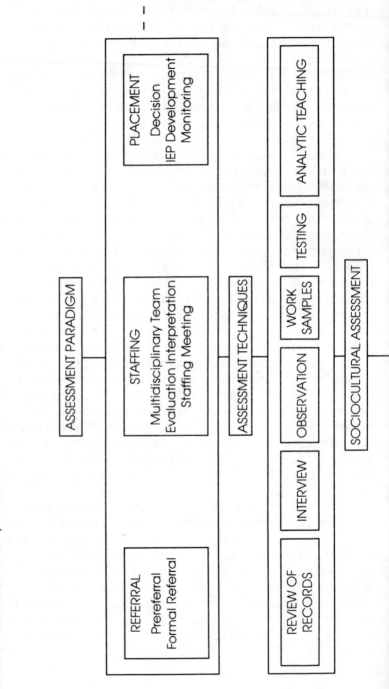

CULTURAL AND LINGUISTIC

EXPERIENTIAL BACKGROUND

LEVEL OF ACCULTUR-ATION

SOCIOLINGUISTIC DEVELOPMENT

COGNITIVE LEARNING STYLES

HYPOTHESIS

Sociocultural factors contributing to learning and behavior problems

Sociocultural factors not contributing to learning and behavior problems

Sociocultural factors and the presence of handicapping conditions contributing to learning and behavior problems

INTERVENTIONS

INDIVIDUALIZED INSTRUCTION PLAN

CONTENT

STRATEGIES

SETTING

REASSESSMENT

Referral

Referral is the first element of the assessment process and the most crucial. Misinterpretation of referral data may have significantly adverse effects upon students, especially those from different cultural backgrounds. Ysseldyke and Algozzine (1982) suggest that the teacher's reason for referral may be a significant factor in the decision to place a student in special education. They found that placement decisions were based primarily upon the teachers' comments about their reasons for referring a student even when the results of academic and behavioral assessment measures did not support those comments. The element of referral in the assessment process is thus an extremely important area of concern.

Referral should include screening as well as the beginning of more in-depth assessment. Many schools now require some form of intervention prior to referral for formal assessment. The overall referral element of assessment includes two types of practices, termed "prereferral intervention" and "formal referral." Prereferral provides an opportunity to gather preliminary information and attempt initial interventions within the regular class setting. Formal referral indicates the need for more complete and comprehensive assessment, based in part on the fact that insufficient progress was made as a result of prereferral interventions.

Prereferral Intervention

The term "prereferral" refers to the time period following an indication by a teacher or a concerned person that the student has some kind of learning or behavior problem (i.e., the student has been referred to a child study team or other person at the building level but before a formal referral for a staffing occurs). A key element of prereferral intervention is the implementation of curricular interventions, prior to formal referral for staffing, which attempt to resolve suspected learning problems.

A minority student may have learning and behavior problems due to language and cultural difference and problems due to a possible handicapping condition. Therefore, one purpose of prereferral interventions in the assessment process is to address the sociocultural needs of the student. Many of the teacher's concerns about the student can be solved by obtaining additional background information. Some problems can be solved with prereferral interventions in the classroom. Figure 3 illustrates the major elements that constitute prereferral intervention.

As shown in Figure 3, the teacher requests assistance and begins gathering information about the student's sociocultural and learning and behavior needs. If current language proficiency information is available and indicates that the student has limited English proficiency, the teacher modifies use of various assessment and intervention techniques to accommodate the student's language and cultural background. The teacher gathers information about the student's background, culture and language, acculturation level, sociolinguistic development and response to the school and classroom environment. She may do this in collaboration with other professionals or with the assistance of a team assigned specifically for this purpose. An example of teacher assistance team activities is discussed at the end of this section.

The areas in which the teacher gathers information include the five sociocultural factors described in Section I: experiential background, cultural and linguistic background, level of acculturation, sociolinguistic development, and cognitive learning styles. The teacher implements a series of interventions to facilitate the collection of this information, and to try out possible resolutions to the student's learning and behavior problems. These interventions are based directly upon the sociocultural factors which may contribute

Figure 3
Prereferral Intervention for Minority Students

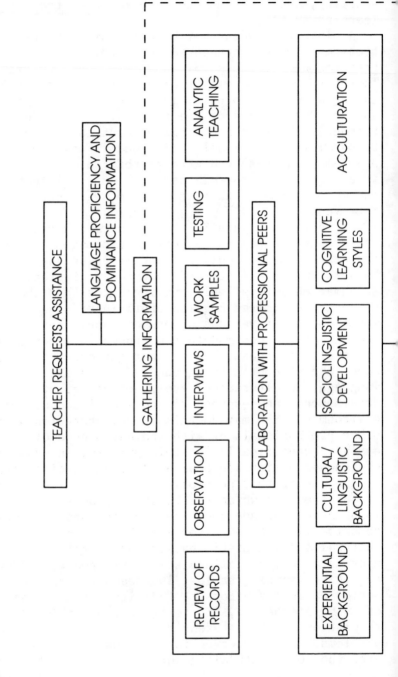

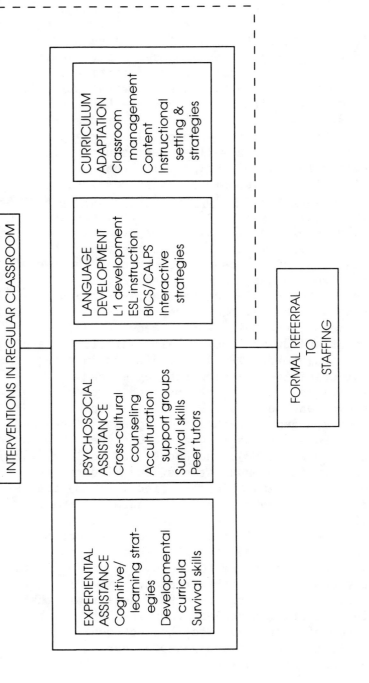

INTERVENTIONS IN REGULAR CLASSROOM

EXPERIENTIAL
ASSISTANCE
Cognitive/
learning strat-
egies
Developmental
curricula
Survival skills

PSYCHOSOCIAL
ASSISTANCE
Cross-cultural
counseling
Acculturation
support groups
Survival skills
Peer tutors

LANGUAGE
DEVELOPMENT
L1 development
ESL instruction
BICS/CALPS
Interactive
strategies

CURRICULUM
ADAPTATION
Classroom
management
Content
Instructional
setting &
strategies

FORMAL REFERRAL
TO
STAFFING

to the minority student's learning and behavior problems. Differences in experiential background and previous school settings may be resolved by providing experiential assistance (e.g., cognitive learning strategies, curricular adaptations, developmental curricula, school survival skills). Differences in cultural and language background and difficulties with the acculturative process may be resolved by providing psychosocial assistance such as cross-cultural counseling, peer support groups, and cultural survival skills. Differences in sociolinguistic development may be resolved by providing language development interventions such as ESL instruction, bilingual assistance, native language development, basic interpersonal communications skills, and cognitive academic language proficiency assistance through the use of interactive language learning strategies.

For further reading on interactive language learning strategies, the reader should consult Slife, Weiss, and Bell (1985), Keogh (1973), Palincsar and Brown (1987), Palincsar (1986), and Collier and Hoover (1987), who discuss in detail the role of cognitive learning strategies as interventions. Waksman, Messmer and Waksman (1988) and Hoover and Collier (1986) review teaching and behavior management techniques. Goodman (1986) and Hakuta (1986) discuss language techniques. Hausman (1988), Hoover (1988), and Hoover and Collier (1986) address curricular adaptations, and Winograd and Niquette (1988) and Shinn and Tindal (1988) discuss other intervention strategies. Figure 3 summarizes prereferral intervention and its relationship to the five sociocultural factors that must be addressed to determine whether the student's learning and behavior problem is due to his or her sociocultural differences, or some other reason.

Ysseldyke and Algozzine (1981) have shown that special education placement when in doubt of the existence of a true handicap has not benefited students; the information gathered during prereferral interventions helps to clarify distinctions between a handicapping condition and sociocultural differences. Prior to a formal referral for a special education staffing, teachers should consider the following variables: (a) time for adjustment, (b) familiarity with the school system and language, and (c) cultural differences.

The student and his family should be permitted enough time to adjust to the new country and environment. The family is probably concerned with such survival items as food, shelter, jobs, communication, and clothing. There may be little time or energy to nurture and support the student. The entire family, especially if refugees, may experience feelings of separation and loss concerning their homeland and other family members. They may suffer the loss of status in occupation because of the need to accept menial or repetitive jobs due to limited English proficiency.

The student needs time (1 1/2 to 2 years) to become proficient in English language basic interpersonal communication skills (BICS). It usually takes from 5 to 7 years for the student to gain cognitive academic language proficiency (CALP) to the level of his American peers. Formal testing in English should not be conducted before the student has had adequate time to learn the language.

Children become proficient in the second language more quickly than adults; often the student becomes the communication link for the family, upsetting the traditional family roles and causing stress within the family unit. Thus, it is appropriate to use a translator when possible to communicate with the family rather than relying on the student. The student needs to learn and adjust to the physical environment, including the climate, the community, and the school. Students may not be accustomed to classes, sitting at desks and doing pencil-paper tasks, and therefore need to learn the routines of the school and the expectations of the teachers. Students need to relate to several different teachers during the day as well as learn to meet their own physical needs when in the school environment.

If the student is literate in the native language, it will be easier to learn English because necessary concepts and vocabulary will have been acquired and learning will be largely a matter of translation. If the student is not literate in the native language, he must learn things in English for which he does not have the concepts or vocabulary in the proficient language. Consequently, learning will be slower and more difficult. Some students may be totally unfamiliar with pencil-paper tasks. Some students may never have had the opportunity or the supplies for writing and may therefore be totally unprepared for pencil-paper tasks. In addition, the limited English proficient student should not be taught to read in English until a good oral language base in English has been established. This may require a year or more of concentrated effort. Teaching a young student to read is not the same as teaching reading to an adult who usually already possesses the language, conceptual constructs, and vocabulary.

All students have the same human need for love, caring, belonging, approval, and achievement. While their cultural and belief systems may differ, students can share them with us, enriching everyone involved. Some cultures don't stress concepts of time; others do not recognize certain colors or express numbers in a manner similar to the majority culture. Rather than viewing these differences as troublesome or as disabilities, the professional should encourage students to share different ways of perceiving the world. All students in the class can benefit from learning to see the world in a new way.

Although a variety of interventions should be tried and pieces of information should be gathered during the prereferral stage, several key elements should be identified and recorded to determine whether a formal referral is justified. These elements include:

1. Establishing the most proficient language in both BICS and CALP.

2. Estimating the level of acculturation and degree of acculturative stress the student is undergoing.

3. Identifying cultural, linguistic, and cognitive style differences.

4. Meeting with parents to discuss the student's problems and eliciting their suggestions to help the student.

5. Implementing several interventions to address suspected learning and behavior problems.

6. Providing ESL instruction and instruction in the student's home language.

7. Using a reasonable waiting and observation period to allow the student sufficient time to adapt to the school environment before formal referral for assessment.

8. Providing vision and hearing exams.

9. Teaching the student basic school survival skills such as how to take tests or how to behave appropriately in school situations.

10. Using criterion-referenced tests to pinpoint specific strengths and weaknesses in both languages.

11. Observing the student interacting with other students, teachers, and parents in the school, the home, and the community in order to identify differences in behavior, language use, and confidence.

After attempting various prereferral interventions

and documenting their results, the teacher may decide that a formal comprehensive evaluation is necessary. Once a formal referral to staffing is made, the legal constraints of P. L. 94-142 regarding staffing and formal assessment must be applied.

Formal Referral

During the prereferral process, pertinent information concerning the student's cultural and linguistic background is obtained. Sociocultural concerns about the student's learning and behavior problems serve to identify specific problem areas that need further evaluation. At the time of formal referral, the referring educator should ensure that all pertinent information gathered during prereferral screening and intervention activities is compiled and available to the multidisciplinary team responsible for the formal evaluation. The initial task of the person(s) who receive the formal referral is to determine whether a comprehensive evaluation is warranted based on the information gathered during the prereferral stage. The person who makes the referral will facilitate the process by succinctly and objectively outlining on the referral form the suspected problem and the information obtained during the prereferral stage. It is important to remember that the reason for referral may be a significant contributing factor in potential placement decisions; the person who makes the referral must ensure that the referral is accurate and relevant. This includes ensuring that sociocultural factors have been considered and found to be invalid as contributing factors to the student's problem. In essence, one purpose of prereferral activities is to gather sufficient information to ascertain the role of sociocultural factors in the exhibited learning and behavior problems. If the referral portion of the assessment process is completed appropriately and a formal referral to staffing is made, the following items will be evident:

1. Sociocultural information that has been compiled suggests whether sociocultural factors are primary contributors to the student's learning or behavior problem or that other factors contribute significantly to the suspected learning and behavior problem;

2. Specific attempts to remedy the problems through the use of appropriate interventions were completed and insufficient progress was made;

3. All information, interventions, and screening data were documented accurately and organized for reference during the formal evaluation; and

4. The decision is made that the minority student's learning and behavior problems are more complex than can be assessed through general screening; more formal comprehensive evaluation is necessary to determine more complete and appropriate forms of remediation.

The next stage of the assessment process, staffing, begins upon completion of referral stage if at that time it is decided that formal comprehensive evaluation is warranted.

Staffing

Staffing involves the formal evaluation and the staffing meeting conducted by the multidisciplinary team in order to review the evaluation results and to determine student eligibility for placement. By the time staffing takes place, the decision to conduct more formal evaluation has already been made. Specifics concerning this formal evaluation are formulated at the staffing meeting. It should also be noted that although formal evaluation is planned, interventions begun during the referral stage should continue and the results of their effectiveness should be documented.

A basic premise of this book is that assessment is the process of gathering meaningful, instructional information about student needs. The question of what is "meaningful" creates some controversy during the interpretation of data. Educators want information related to the classroom learning environment, to students' learning and behavior problems within that environment, and to particular circumstances in which students can perform learning tasks successfully. Knowing when, how, and in what way a student can do something helps in planning for success, effective teaching, and optimal learning. Educators are also concerned with the collection of information related to students' socioeconomic background, home environment, and other out-of-school experiences. Two key elements to consider during staffing of culturally and linguistically different students are (a) the skills of the multidisciplinary team and (b) the appropriateness and the comprehensiveness of the interpretation of evaluation findings.

Multidisciplinary Team

The multidisciplinary team is constrained by the regulations of P. L. 94-142, which do not apply during prereferral. These include signed approval forms, required presence of parents, and specific timelines for completion of the assessment process. As a result of these concerns, the multidisciplinary team usually involves members whose primary function is to determine an appropriate special education placement in the least restrictive environment. Multidisciplinary teams must address the special needs of culturally and linguistically different students who are also handicapped; therefore, they should be composed of educators who can respond to these special needs. The multidisciplinary team is only as effective as the skills and competencies of its members, and individuals involved in the assessment of minority students should possess several competencies to ensure the attainment of the most meaningful and accurate information. Baca and Cervantes (in press) and Jones (1988) discuss the type of skills needed by multidisciplinary team members involved in the assessment of minority students. In addition to the usual range of abilities found on the multidisciplinary team (e.g., teacher, psychologist, social worker, school nurse, diagnostician), one or more members of the team must also possess the following skills:

1. Knowledge of the appropriate use of instruments and procedures to assess language proficiency and first and second language abilities.

2. Knowledge of the principles to select a measure designed for use with students from the target populations, including but not limited to consideration of reliability, validity, norms, standards for administration, interpretation of outcomes, and sources of cultural bias.

3. Knowledge of limitations of language assessment that result from examiner role, testing situation, content selection, questioning, dialect varieties of the target language, use of interpretation, and social-emotional factors.

4. Ability to apply the information from testing, observations, and parent and teacher interviews to identify (a) baseline levels of skills and comprehension, (b) conditions under which skill acquisition can occur most efficiently, (c) the sequence of instructional activities needed, and (d) a plan for evaluation of both process and performance objectives.

5. Knowledge and application of appropriate collaboration skills related to working with educational staff and parents in planning and

implementing individual educational plans for
minority pupils demonstrating exceptionality.

6. Ability to devise or adapt existing instruments
   for assessing minority pupils, which may include
   (a) developing new normative data appropriate to
   the population and (b) developing informal
   instruments appropriate to the population.

7. Knowledge of factors which influence second
   language acquisition, including use, motivation,
   attitude, personality, cognition, and the first
   language.

8. Knowledge of the cognitive and language
   development of a normally developing minority
   student.

9. Knowledge of cultural factors, including
   semantic and pragmatic systems, as they relate
   to sociolinguistic environment (i.e.,
   parent-student, school-student interaction).

10. Knowledge of the dynamics of the interpretation
    procedure, including but not limited to the
    establishment of rapport with participants,
    kinds of information loss inherent in the
    interpretation procedure, the use of appropriate
    nonverbal communication, methods and techniques
    of interpretation, the importance of obtaining
    accurate translations, the need to procure
    translations that do not reflect personal
    evaluations of the person whose remarks are
    being interpreted, and efforts to minimize the
    interpreter's elaborated responses or questions.

11. Ability to plan and execute pre- and
    postassessment conferences.

   An additional competency related to item 10 above
is the ability of the multidisciplinary team to
decide whether the services of an interpreter are

necessary. An interpreter can translate the test or other assessment techniques, prepare student and parents for the assessment process, interpret student responses, and facilitate communication with the parents during the staffing meeting. An interpreter may be necessary when a bilingual professional is not available, when it is inappropriate to have a peer or sibling translate, when the student is not literate in his dominant language, or when no tests are available in the student's dominant language. It is important to remember that the ability to speak a language well and the ability to translate are two distinct skills and are not necessarily found in all bilingual persons. Professionals may need training to work effectively with interpreters.

Among the skills needed by professionals who utilize the services of interpreters is the ability to plan and execute pre- and postdiagnostic conferences with the interpreter. In these conferences, the school professional trains and orients the interpreter to the purposes and procedures appropriate to formal testing, interviews, observations, and other assessment activities. To be able to do this effectively, school personnel need to be familiar with the dynamics of the interpretation process which include establishing rapport with participants, being familiar with methods and techniques in the field of interpetation and translation, being knowledgeable about the use of appropriate nonverbal communication, and being aware of the loss of information (such as omissions, additions, and substitutions) inherent in the interpretation process. Perhaps the most important skill a school professional needs when working with an interpreter is the ability to work with the interpreter, being able to ensure trust between the person conducting the assessment and the interpreter, knowing how to record the behavior of the interpreter in testing situations, and being able to effectively convey information to the interpreter so an accurate translation can be facilitated. Training of interpreters is an ongoing process that takes into account the current activities of the school assessment personnel.

Implicit in the above skills is knowing what kind of training the interpreters need. The key is to provide training before student testing and to review after testing. Translating, especially in an evaluative capacity, can be a very difficult task, and usually requires training for the interpreter in all phases of assessment since the interpreter should be involved in the total assessment process including test modification. The translation of a test instrument or any other material may be checked for validity by having another bilingual translate the text back into English.

In addition to a high level of competency in all four language skills (listening, speaking, reading, writing), the interpreter should have some understanding of student development, language variation (dialects, language domains, registers), and cross-cultural variables. Interpreters need training in the administration of tests, including how to transmit information about role playing, how to cue a student during assessment, how to prompt for responses, and how to probe for pertinent information or responses. Training in confidentiality is also essential. The competence and expertise will vary among interpreters, but what is essential in this important position is a highly developed sense of professional responsibility.

The skills of the multidisciplinary team are the first component of staffing. The inclusion of someone with skills in cross-cultural communication and interpretation is necessary in the assessment of minority students. The second component of staffing of minority students is the interpretation of evaluation results.

Evaluation Interpretation

Hammill (1987) notes that assessment results are

merely observations of behavior which must be interpreted to give them meaning. The interpretation of evaluation data has been discussed in detail in Section II. However, during the staffing process, the results of the evaluations conducted by team members must be interpreted in light of prereferral information and student performance during formal evaluation. This requires the modification of the interpretation process in order to address sociocultural concerns.

One method of modifying the interpretation process is the use of videotaping (conducted in the least obtrusive manner possible). Student and examiner can be videotaped as they interact on a particular test or procedure. The entire multidisciplinary team will then be able to observe and comment on the results. Videotaping allows the team access to norm-referenced, criterion-referenced, and nonreferenced interpretation. In addition, members of the team who may be more familiar with the student's culture and language have the opportunity to comment on how these factors impact directly on student performance. Viewing the tape is helpful when discussing assessment results with parents.

Another method of modifying the interpretation process is to change the scoring and interpretation of test results. This procedure, outlined in Table 6, includes reviewing the test before administration to identify possibly biased or questionable items, modifying the interpretation of student errors, rescoring potentially biased items, and comparing the results of alternative scoring. If the rescoring shows little difference in performance, further student assessment is needed to determine eligibility for placement in special education. However, the influence of sociocultural factors should not be ruled out. If the rescoring shows moderate difference in performance, the student may need further eligibility assessment and programming that will address language and acculturation needs. If the rescoring shows considerable difference in

Table 6
Recommendations for Scoring Standardized Tests

1. Determine specifically what you wish to know.

2. Select a test that examines the knowledge or skill that needs to be assessed.

3. Determine if it was designed to be administered to the student's cultural/linguistic group.

4. Choose a test that has the most appropriate and valid items for the knowledge or skill being assessed.

5. Examine each item or illustration before administering the test to determine whether the student has had access to the information necessary to respond to it.

6. Modify inappropriate items or illustrations.

7. First administer the test according to the manual, recording the student's complete response.

8. If the student misses items previously identified as possibly inappropriate, reword your instructions and provide additional time for the student to respond.

9. Continue testing beyond the ceiling unless the student is clearly at his or her threshold.

10. Provide positive feedback after every response.

11. Record all of the students responses and allow the student to change his or her mind if it is clear that he or she knows the answers.

12. Compare the student's responses with the ones considered to be correct on the test. Give credit for very similar responses.

13. When items are found to be incorrect according to the manual, compare them with reported dialect and linguistic features of the student's language. If the responses are correct according to the linguistic rules of his language, record a second set of scores with these items marked correct.

14. First, score the test as directed in the manual. Even though you may have modified some items, compare the responses according to the rules of the test. Next, rescore each item, allowing credit for those items that are considered correct in the student's language and culture.

15. Compare both sets of scores with the norms. The modified scores will probably be higher than those scored "by the book." However, students who are truly handicapped in the area being assessed will score low no matter how the test is scored. If the modified score is significantly higher than the other, the student is likely to have the knowledge or skill being tested, but may need instruction in transferring that knowledge or skill to the second language and culture.

16. When reporting the results of this test, indicate where the adjustments were made in the protocol, content, and scoring. Be sure to describe what was done, and the differences in the student's responses after each modification.

performance, the student may need language and acculturation assistance. However, possible handicapping conditions cannot be ruled out as a factor in learning and behavior problems. All assessment results must be considered by the multidisciplinary team during the staffing meeting, including considerations of prereferral intervention information, evaluation of sociocultural indicators, and evaluation of specific learning and behavior problems.

Staffing Meeting

During the staffing meeting, the team discusses the results of the evaluations and determines if the minority student is eligible for placement in special education. As illustrated in Figure 2, three hypotheses are tested during the meeting: (a) the student's learning and behavior problems are primarily due to sociocultural factors, (b) the student's problems are primarily due to a handicapping condition, and (c) the student's problems are primarily due to a combination of sociocultural factors and a handicapping condition. The team must share and discuss the findings of their evaluations of the student, the results of the prereferral interventions implemented with the student, the formal referral information, and any other information pertinent to each hypothesis. Analyzing hypotheses during the staffing meeting leads to placement decisions.

Placement

Placement decisions are made at the conclusion of the staffing meeting. Resolution of the three hypotheses is the foundation for placement and takes into account sociocultural factors and assessment techniques.

Decision

If the multidisciplinary team finds that the minority student's learning and behavior problems are due primarily to sociocultural factors, the decision may be to return the student to the general education program with recommendations for addressing these sociocultural needs. If the team decides that the minority student's learning and behavior problems are not due to sociocultural factors, they may identify the nature of his or her specific learning and behavior problems, and recommend special education placement. They may also recommend placement in special education if they determine that the minority student's problems are due to a combination of sociocultural factors and the presence of a handicapping condition. In the latter two cases, the team may develop an IEP which addresses all of the minority student's special needs, including sociocultural.

IEP Development

The individualized educational plan (IEP) is developed after the placement decision is made. It is usually based on a determination of the student's strengths and weaknesses in the areas of achievement, aptitude/ability, and emotional/behavioral competence. In addition to identifying the student's general competence in these areas, an IEP specifies instructional objectives and a sequence of actions for achieving these objectives through modification of the instructional content, strategies, and setting.

The IEP, developed in consultation with all concerned parties, must be a comprehensive presentation of the student's total learning needs. This includes instructional guidelines and objectives to address the student's acculturation and language acquisition needs, as well as his special educational needs. In addition, it should address the integration of these services,

indicating who is responsible for providing and
maintaining culturally and linguistically
appropriate instructional interventions. The IEP
should also address how culturally and
linguistically appropriate instructional
interventions will be utilized in meeting the
student's special needs. The steps involved in IEP
development for minority students with special needs
include the development of objectives related to (a)
native language development and English language
acquisition, (b) the facilitation of acculturation,
(c) special education, (d) the integration of
specific culture and language interventions which
address special education needs, (e) identification
of service providers responsible for implementing
and monitoring the integration of these services,
and (f) the time limits and scheduled specific
reevaluation formats, dates, and meetings.

Monitoring

The final element in the placement procedure is
monitoring. As illustrated in Figure 2, assessment
is a cyclical process. As prescriptions and
interventions are implemented within the assessment
process, student responses are monitored on an
ongoing basis. The IEP contains a projected schedule
for monitoring and subsequent reassessment of the
minority handicapped student's learning and behavior
problems.

The plan for monitoring should indicate the
individual responsible for each element of the
monitoring process and should include (a) regular
assessment of the handicapped student's second
language acquisition, (b) periodic review of his or
her degree of acculturation and response to
acculturative stress, and (c) monitoring the
student's changing response to the school
environment and to the acquisition of new cognitive
learning strategies. Depending upon the minority
handicapped student's response to sociocultural
prescriptions and interventions, and to those

prescribed to address the student's learning and behavior problem, the monitoring process may result in reassessing the placement decision and the student's return to the general education program. On the other hand, as the minority handicapped student successfully resolves the identified learning and behavior problems, additional problems may be manifested. In this case, monitoring would result in a reassessment of the student's needs and a subsequent revision of the IEP. Monitoring is the final component of the placement stage and completes the total assessment process for minority students.

Future Concerns

Although numerous issues were discussed throughout this book, there are several concerns of increasing importance in the assessment and subsequent instruction of minority students. Four of these are the development of teacher assistance teams as part of prereferral intervention, the continuing debate about the use of standardized tests with minority students, the increasing number of students from non-Hispanic language and culture backgrounds, and the complexities of mainstreaming these diverse populations.

Teacher Assistance Child Intervention Team

There is a consensus among bilingual special educators (Collier, 1987; Ortiz & Garcia, 1988) that the time between initial teacher referral and staffing should be used for intervention strategies which would facilitate more appropriate diagnosis of the student's real needs. Prereferral interventions may be accomplished by reallocating time and resources, and can be expanded through greater access to multidisciplinary personnel. This could result in a Teacher Assistance Child Intervention Team (TACIT) created by expanding an existing child study team or another group of professionals who provide assistance to teachers who work with

culturally and linguistically different students
with concomitant learning and behavior problems.

Intervention strategies that address the
culturally and linguistically different student's
language acquisition, language development, and
acculturation needs, enable the TACIT and the
classroom teacher to sort out with greater
confidence the learning and behavior problems caused
by a handicapping condition and the problems due to
acculturation experience and language acquisition
needs. By documenting the student's performance and
response to the prereferral interventions suggested
by the TACIT, preliminary diagnostic judgments can
be made about the student's need for further
intervention and/or formal referral to staffing.

The team not only reviews the classroom teacher's
specific concerns about the student, but also makes
suggestions for modifying the learning environment
for the student within the regular classroom and
provides guidance, training, and assistance in
implementing the intervention suggestions. Local and
central school administration must support the roles
of the team members in prereferrals, referrals, and
staffing and must provide them with adequate time
for planning and consultation. The TACIT can assure
compliance with legal guidelines, relieves the
staffing team of some time in separating cultural,
linguistic, and acculturation variables from special
educational variables that impact the assessment,
and alleviates the staffing process at the
prereferral level.

The TACIT that assists the teacher in diagnostic
intervention during the prereferral period should be
composed of the student's parents or student
advocate and professionals who are knowledgeable
about special and remedial education techniques and
strategies, acculturation process and cross-cultural
instructional strategies, the cultural and language
background of the student, and bilingual/ESL
resources and instructional strategies. Teachers,
school psychologists, support staff, principals, and
social workers who are bilingual or familiar with

86

diverse cultures are all potential TACIT team members. The composition of the TACIT can represent a multicultural population with members who serve only when referred students belong to their particular cultural or linguistic groups. Selection of TACIT members should not be accomplished by any one method but should include self selection and peer selection.

To establish a viable TACIT, administrative support must be obtained, an awareness of team functioning among school personnel must be developed, team selection must include the participation of the entire school, and all school personnel must receive inservice training about the TACIT and its function. The TACIT must meet regularly, and, above all, the efforts of the school and TACIT must be consistent and persistent in meeting the special needs of culturally and linguistically different learners.

Use of Standardized Norm-Referenced Tests

The composition of the population used for norming a test is the major concern in using standardized norm-referenced tests when assessing minority students. The test designer must decide which population will provide the norms for the varied sociocultural populations examined. If, for example, a test designer's decision about establishing norms causes the test scores of one sociocultural group to be consistently higher or lower than those of another sociocultural group, the norm-referenced test may be biased against the sociocultural group obtaining consistently lower test scores. When norm-referenced instruments are based on experiences unfamiliar to students from a sociocultural group, the rights of these students must be protected.

The Larry P. v. Wilson Riles case of 1979 exemplifies the concern about the use of standardized norm-referenced tests in the assessment of minority students. The case, begun in 1970, was a class action suit against the San Francisco Unified School District and the California State Department of Education on behalf of black students who were allegedly misclassified as educable mentally retarded (EMR) based on invalid IQ test results. The case challenged the construct validity of standardized IQ tests as a measure of the learning potential of minority students. As a result of the Larry P. case, California banned the use of standardized IQ tests for the assessment of minority students for special education purposes.

The implications of this case extend far beyond testing for special education. Any use of an IQ test is prohibited if such assessment could lead to special education placement or services, even if the test is part of a comprehensive assessment plan. Since the case was based on bias inherent in standardization, norm-referenced interpretation, and content, it has far-reaching implications for the continued use of standardized norm-referenced tests with all culturally and linguistically different students.

Non-Hispanic Minority Populations

Educators have improved the assessment of and instruction for Hispanics, who constitute the largest minority population in the United States. The number of Spanish-speaking teachers, school psychologists, superintendents, and other education personnel has increased significantly. However, the educational system has not addressed adequately the needs of the rapidly growing minority Asian and other non-Hispanic populations. There are very few education professionals proficient in the languages of these populations. The diversity of these cultures, which often are linked only by geographical origin, makes the problem even more complex.

Although it is highly probable that a bilingual educator or a bilingual special educator fluent in Spanish can work effectively with Spanish speaking students, such bilingual personnel probably do not possess the linguistic skills to work effectively with a group of Spanish, Hmong, Laotian, Vietnamese, Chinese, Navajo, and Persian students. Training in cross-cultural communication skills in addition to sensitivity and the development of multicultural instructional environments is critical. It would be ideal to have school personnel who speak the native languages of the students or to have access to individuals who are fluent in those languages. The current dearth of multilingual and multicultural professionals in our schools is clearly a concern that must be addressed.

Mainstreaming

Mainstreaming remains a problem for handicapped students regardless of their cultural and linguistic background. Teachers often lack sufficient preparation to deal with many handicapping conditions and less so to work with cultural and linguistically different students. Indeed, many minority student referrals for special education services occur because teachers cannot assist these students, and may find their presence disruptive in the classroom learning environment (Collier, 1985; Hoover & Collier, 1985). Although teacher training is one way to address the problem, cross-cultural education is not yet an institutionalized component of teacher preparation programs. Many universities have been slow to integrate this specialized training into their teacher training programs. School districts have also been slow in developing integrated delivery procedures which could accommodate, within the regular program, all the special needs of their students. As we consider future concerns related to the education of minority students with learning and behavior problems, mainstreaming issues will continue to confront educators at all levels of our educational system.

Points for Discussion - Section III

1. List two factors likely to increase the probability of successful prereferral interventions.

2. List the major components of a well-designed prereferral intervention program.

3. Identify the major components of a systematic assessment process for minority students.

4. Outline the process of establishing a TACIT.

5. Describe a comprehensive assessment program for a particular minority student.

Summary

Assessing minority students with learning and behavior problems has explored three important areas related to the assessment of minority students who may be handicapped. They are: (a) sociocultural considerations, (b) assessment techniques, and (c) ways of adapting the assessment process to facilitate effective and appropriate placement decisions. Five important sociocultural factors were explored; six assessment techniques were discussed in detail, and numerous examples were provided to illustrate their proper use. The adaptation of the assessment process presented in this book will assist professionals to make appropriate instruction and placement decisions. Through the identification of specific sociocultural factors which may contribute to the student's learning and behavior problems, and modifications of the assessment process, the teacher is best able to plan and implement instruction which provides learners an opportunity to acquire information which is compatible with their own individual needs. It is the author's hope that the contents of this book encourage educators to obtain instructionally meaningful information about the needs of culturally and linguistically different students. Adoption of the procedures recommended will improve the quality of education for all students from diverse cultural and linguistic backgrounds.

References

Adler, P. S. (1975). The transitional experience: An alternative view of culture shock. Journal of Humanistic Psychology, 15, 13–23.

Albino-Cordero, H. P. (1981). An investigation of the effects of bilingualism and non-bilingual school programs on pupil adjustment. Unpublished doctoral dissertation, University of Connecticut.

Allen, J. P. & Van Buren, P. (Eds.). (1971). Chomsky: Selected readings. London: Oxford University Press.

American Psychological Association. (1985). Standards for educational and psychological testing. Washington, D.C.: American Educational Research Association, American Psychological Association.

Argulewicz, E. D., & Elliott, S. N. (1981, August). Validity of the SRBCSS for Hispanic and gifted students. Paper presented at the meeting of the American Psychological Association, Los Angeles.

Baca, L. M., & Cervantes, H. T. (in press). The bilingual special education interface (2d ed.). Columbus, OH: Merrill.

Berry, J. W. (1970). Marginality, stress, and ethnic identification in an acculturated aboriginal community. Journal of Cross Cultural Psychology, 1, 239–252.

Berry, J. W. (1976). Human ecology and cognitive style: Comparative studies in cultural psychological adaptation. New York: Sage/Halstead.

Berry, J. W. (1980). Acculturation as varieties of adaptation. In A. M. Padilla, Acculturation:

Theory, models, and some new findings (pp. 9–27).
American Association for the Advancement of
Science Symposium Series 39. Boulder, CO:
Westview Press.

Blumenthal, A. L. (1977). *The process of cognition*.
Englewood Cliffs, NJ: Prentice-Hall.

Brigance, A. H. (1978). *Diagnostic Inventory of
Basic Skills*. North Billerica, MN: Curriculum
Associates.

Brown, L. (1987). Assessing socioemotional
development. In D. D. Hammill (Ed.), *Assessing
the abilities and instructional needs of students*
(pp. 504–609). Austin, TX: Pro-Ed.

Butler, K. G., Bernstein, D. K., & Seidenberg, P. L.
(1988). Language and cognitive processing: Issues
for assessment and intervention, [Special Issue].
Topics in Language Disorders, 8.

California Department of Education (in press). *Guide
to alternative assessment: Larry P. Task Force
Report*. Sacramento: Author.

Chesarek, S. (1981, March). *Cognitive consequences
of home or school education in a limited second
language: A case study in the Crow indian
bilingual community*. Paper presented at the
Language Proficiency Assessment Symposium, Airlie
House, Virginia.

Collier, C. (1985). A comparison of acculturation
and education characteristics of referred and
nonreferred culturally and linguistically
different children. *Dissertation Abstracts
International, 46*, 2993A.

Collier, C. (1987). Bilingual special education
curriculum training. Proceedings of the
Cross-Cultural Special Education Network

Symposium (pp. 12–43). Denver: University of
Colorado.

Collier, C., & Hoover, J. J. (1987). <u>Cognitive
learning strategies for minority handicapped
students.</u> Lindale, TX: Hamilton Publications.

Commins, N. (1986). <u>A descriptive study of the
linguistic abilities of four low-achieving
hispanic bilingual students.</u> Unpublished doctoral
dissertation, University of Colorado, Boulder.

Cummins, J. (1984). <u>Bilingualism and special
education: Issues in assessment and pedagogy.</u>
Avon, England: Multilingual Matters.

Cummins, J. (1986). The role of primary language
development in promoting educational success for
language minority students. In <u>Schooling and
language minority students: A theoretical
framework</u> (pp. 3–51). Los Angeles: California
State Department of Education, Evaluation,
Dissemination, and Assistance Center, California
State University at Los Angeles, 11th printing.

Curtiss, S. (1982). Developmental dissociation of
language and cognition. In K. Obler and E. Menes
(Eds.), <u>Exceptional language and linguistics</u> (pp.
139–159). New York: Academic Press.

DeAvila, E., & Duncan, S. (1986). <u>Language
assessment scales (LAS).</u> Corte Madero, CA:
Linguametrics.

Duran, R. P. (in preparation). An assessment program
for Hispanic students referred for special
education testing. University of California,
Santa Barbara.

Elliott, S., & Bretzing, B. (1980). Local norms.
<u>Psychology in the Schools</u>, <u>17</u>, 195–201.

Epstein, H. T. (1978). Growth spurts during brain development: Implications for educational policy and practice. In J. Chall and A. Mirsky (Eds.), Education and the brain (pp. 343-370). Chicago: University of Chicago Press.

Feuerstein, R. (1982). Learning potential assessment device (LPAD). Baltimore, MD: University Park Press.

Figueroa, R. A. (1986). Test bias and Hispanic children. The Journal of Special Education. 17, 431-440.

Finn, J. D. (1982). Patterns in special education placement as revealed by the OCR surveys. In K. A. Heller, W. H. Holtzman & S. Messick (Eds.), Placing children in special education: A strategy for equity (pp. 322-381). Washington, DC: National Academy Press.

Gardner, R. W., Jackson, D. N., and Messick, S. J. (1960). Personality organization in cognitive controls and intellectual abilities. Psychological Issues, 2, 1-149.

Goodenough, W. H. (1957). Cultural anthropology and linguistics. In P. Garvin (Ed.), Report of the 7th annual meeting on linguistics and language study (Monograph Series on Language and Linguistics, No. 9, pp. 167-173). Washington, D. C.: Georgetown University.

Goodman, K. (1986) What's whole in whole language. Portsmouth, NH: Heineman Educational Books.

Goodman, Y., & Burke, C. L. (1972). Reading miscue inventory. New York: Macmillan.

Gronlund, N. E. (1985). Measurement and evaluation in teaching. (5th edition). New York: Macmillan.

Grosjean, F. (1982). Life with two languages: An introduction to bilingualism. Cambridge, MA: Harvard University Press.

Hakuta, K. (1986). Mirror of language: The debate on bilingualism. New York: Basic Books.

Hakuta, K., & Diaz, R. (1984). The relationship between the degree of bilingualism and cognitive ability: A critical discussion and some longitudinal data. In K. E. Nelson (Ed.), Children's language (pp. 5-15). Hillsdale, NJ: Erlbaum.

Hammill, D. D. (1987). Assessing the abilities and instructional needs of students. Austin, TX: Pro-Ed.

Hammill, D. D., Brown, L., & Bryant, B. (1987). A consumer's guide to tests in print. Austin, TX: Pro-Ed.

Hausman, R. M. (1988). Adaptation of the learning potential assessment strategy to special education diagnostic classroom settings. In R. L. Jones (Ed.), Psychoeducational assessment of minority group children: A casebook (pp. 305-317). Berkeley, CA: Cobb & Henry.

Haywood, H. C. (1988). Dynamic assessment: The learning potential device. In R. L. Jones (Ed.), Psychoeducational assessment of minority group children: A casebook (pp. 39-64). Berkeley, CA: Cobb & Henry.

Heller, K. A., Holtzman, W. H., & Messick, S. (Eds.). (1982). Placing children in special education: A strategy for equity. Washington, DC: National Academy Press.

Hoover, J. J. (1988). <u>Curriculum adaptation for</u>
<u>students with learning and behavior problems</u>.
Lindale, TX: Hamilton Publications.

Hoover, J. J., & Collier, C. (1985). Referring
culturally different children for special
education: Sociocultural considerations. <u>Academic</u>
<u>Therapy</u>, <u>20</u>, 503-510.

Hoover, J. J., & Collier, C. (1986). <u>Classroom</u>
<u>management through curricular adaptations:</u>
<u>Educating minority handicapped students</u>. Lindale,
TX: Hamilton Publications.

Idol, L., Nevin, A., & Paolucci-Whitcomb, P. (1986).
<u>Models of curriculum-based assessment</u>. Austin,
TX: Pro-Ed.

Jones, R. L. (1988). <u>Psychoeducational assessment of</u>
<u>minority group children: A casebook</u>. Berkeley,
CA: Cobb & Henry.

Juffer, K. A. (1983). Initial development and
validation of an instrument to access degree of
culture shock adaptation. In R. J. Bransford
(Ed.), <u>Monograph Series</u>, <u>4</u>, 136-149. BUENO Center
for Multicultural Education, Boulder, CO.

Kaufman, A. S., & Kaufman, N. L. (1983). <u>(K-ABC):</u>
<u>Assessment battery for children</u>. Circle Pines,
MN: American Guidance Service.

Keogh, B. K. (1973). Perceptual and cognitive
styles: Implications for special education. In L.
Mann & D. Sabatino (Eds.), <u>The first review of</u>
<u>special education</u>. Philadelphia: JSE Press.

<u>Keymath: Diagnostic arithmetic test</u>. (1976). Circle
Pines, MN: American Guidance Service.

Knoff, H. H. (1983). Effect of diagnostic

information on special education placement decisions. Exceptional Children, 49, 440-444.

Lau v. Nichols. (1974). 414 U.S. 563; 39 L.Ed 2d 1, 94 S. Ct. 786.

Leiter, R. G. (1976). Leiter international performance scale (LIPS-AA). Chicago, IL: Stoelting.

Lenneberg, E. H. (1967). Biological foundations of language. New York: Wiley.

Mann, L., & Sabatino, D. A. (1985). Foundations of cognitive process in remedial and special education. Austin, TX: Pro-Ed.

McLoughlin, J. A., & Lewis, R. B. (1986). Assessing special students. Columbus, OH: Merrill.

Mercer, J. R. (1984). What is a racially and culturally nondiscriminatory test? A sociological and pluralistic perspective. In C. R. Reynolds & R. T. Brown (Eds.), Perspectives on bias in mental testing (pp. 293-346). New York: Plenum Press.

Nazarro, J. N. (Ed.). (1981). Culturally diverse exceptional children. Reston, VA: Council for Exceptional Children.

Oakland, T. (1981). Nondiscriminatory assessment. Minneapolis: National School Psychology Training Network.

Omark, D. R., & Watson, D. L. (1984). Assessment of bilingual special education students. San Diego: Los Amigos Research Associates.

Ortiz, A. A., & Garcia, S. (1988). Prereferral teacher assistance model. Proceedings of Cross-Cultural Special Education Network

Symposium, (pp. 10-15). Denver, CO: University of Colorado.

Ortiz, A. A., & Polyzoi, S. (Eds.). (1986). Characteristics of limited English proficient Hispanic students in programs for the learning disabled: Implications for policy, practice, and research. Austin, TX: University of Texas, Handicapped Minority Research Institute on Language Proficiency.

Ortiz, A. A., & Yates, J. R. (1984). Staffing and the development of individualized education programs for bilingual exceptional students. In L. M. Baca & H. T. Cervantes, The bilingual special education interface (pp. 187-213). Columbus, OH: Merrill.

Padilla, A. (Ed.). (1980). Acculturation: Theory, models, and some new findings. American Association for the Advancement of Science Symposium Series 39. Boulder, CO: Westview Press.

Palincsar, A. S. (1986). Metacognitive strategy instruction. Exceptional Children, 53, 118-125.

Palincsar, A. S., & Brown, A. L. (1987). Enhancing instructional time through attention to metacognition. Journal of Learning Disabilities, 20, 66-75.

Ramirez, M., & Castaneda, A. (1974). Cultural democracy: Bicognitive development and education. New York: Academic Press.

Ramirez, M. III, Castaneda, A., & Herold, P. L. (1974). The relationship of acculturation to cognitive style among Mexican-Americans. Journal of Cross-Cultural Psychology. 5, 424-433.

Rueda, R., & Mercer, J. (1985). A predictive analysis for decision making practices with LEP

handicapped students. Paper presented at the
Third Annual Symposium for Bilingual Special
Education, Evaluation, and Research, May.
Northglenn, CO.

Salvia, J., & Ysseldyke, J. E. (1988). Assessment of
special and remedial education (3rd ed.). Boston:
Houghton Mifflin.

Saville-Troike, M. (1983). An anthropological
linguistic perspective on uses of ethnography in
bilingual language proficiency assessment. In C.
Rivera (Ed.), An ethnographic/sociolinguistic
approach to language proficiency assessment
(Multilingual Matters, No.8, pp. 131-136).
Rossyln, VA: InterAmerican Associates.

Seidenberg, P. L. (1988). Cognitive and academic
instructional intervention for learning-disabled
adolescents. Topics in Language Disorders, 8,
56-71.

Serrano, V. Z. (1982). Migrant handicapped children:
A second look at their special education needs
(Report for the Education Commission of the
States). Washington, DC: Education Improvement
Center.

Shinn, M. R., & Tindal, G. A. (1988). Using student
performance data in academics: A pragmatic and
defensible approach to nondiscriminatory
assessment. In R. L. Jones (Ed.),
Psychoeducational assessment of minority group
children: A casebook (pp. 383-411). Berkeley, CA:
Cobb & Henry.

Skutnabb-Kangas, T., & Toukamaa, P. (1976). Teaching
migrant children's mother tongue and learning the
language of the host country in the context of
the sociocultural situation of the migrant
family. Helsinki: UNESCO.

Slife, B. D., Weiss, J., & Bell, T. (1985).
Separability of metacognition and cognition:
Problem solving in learning disabled and regular
students. Journal of Educational Psychology, 77,
437-445.

Slobin, D. I. (1979). Psycholinguistics. New York:
Scott, Foresman.

Snow, C. E. (1984). Parent-child interaction. In R.
L. Schiefelbusch & J. Pickar (Eds.), The
acquisition of communicative competence (Language
Intervention Series, No. 8, pp. 70-107).
Baltimore: University Park Press.

Stone, C. A., & Wertsch, J. V. (1984). A social
interactional analysis of learning disabilities
remediation. Journal of Learning Disabilities,
17, 194-198.

Szapocznik, J., & Kurtines, W. (1980).
Acculturation, biculturalism, and adjustment
among Cuban Americans. In A. Padilla (Ed.),
Acculturation: Theory, models, and some new
findings. (American Association for the
Advancement of Science Symposium Series 39, pp.
139-160). Boulder, CO: Westview Press.

Taylor, J. M. (1988). Behavioral assessment and
special education evaluation: A successful and
necessary marriage. In R. L. Jones (Ed.),
Psychoeducational assessment of minority group
children: A casebook (pp. 225-239). Berkeley, CA:
Cobb & Henry.

United States District Court of Northern California.
(1979). Larry P. v. Wilson Riles. No. C-71-2270
FRP.

Waksman, S., Messmer, C. L., & Waksman, D. D.
(1988). The Waksman social skills curriculum: An
assertive behavior program for adolescents.

Portland, OR: Applied Systems: Instruction
Evaluation Publishing Education.

Wells, C. G. (1981). Learning through interaction:
The study of language development. Cambridge,
England: Cambridge University Press.

Wiederholt, J. L. (1985). Formal reading inventory.
Austin, TX: Pro-Ed.

Wiederholt, J. L., Hammill, D. D., & Brown, V.
(1983). The resource teacher. Austin, TX: Pro-Ed.

Winograd, P., & Niquette, G. (1988). Assessing
learned helplessness in poor readers. Topics in
Language Disorders, 8, 33-54.

Woodcock, J. (1987). Language proficiency battery.
McAllen, TX: DLM/Teaching Resources.

Woodward, M. M. (1981). Indiana experiences with
limited English proficient students: Primarily
with Indochinese refugee children. Report to the
Indiana Department of Public Instruction.
Indianapolis, IN: Indiana Department of Public
Instruction.

Ysseldyke, J. E., & Algozzine, B. (1981). Diagnostic
classification in decisions as a function of
referral information. Journal of Special
Education, 15, 429-435.

Ysseldyke, J. E.,& Algozzine, B. (1982). Critical
issues in special and remedial education. Boston,
MA: Houghton Mifflin.

Ysseldyke, J. E., Algozzine, B., Richey, L. S., &
Graden, J. (1982). Declaring students eligible
for learning disabilities services: Why bother
with the data? Learning Disability Quarterly, 5,
37-44.

About the Author

Catherine Collier received her PhD in 1985 from the University of Colorado, Boulder, specializing in Multicultural/Special Education. She has taught exceptional Native American students in grades K-12 and has developed and administered programs for Navajo and Eskimo students. Dr. Collier has also developed and administered several teacher training programs in bilingual and special education. She has authored and co-authored several chapters, books, and articles in the area of education for culturally and linguistically different exceptional learners. She is presently developing a prereferral intervention program in software format for use with culturally diverse populations. Dr. Collier is Assistant Professor, Adjunct, at the University of Colorado, Boulder, and is the Director of the Bilingual Special Education Curriculum Training (BISECT) Project.